BE A MASTER® OF CHANNELING SPIRIT

CONNECT TO YOUR DIVINE GUIDES & ANGEL PROTECTORS

Dr. Theodoros Kousouli

A Personal Empowerment Book

Kousouli Enterprises
Los Angeles, CA

Copyright © 2018 by Theodoros Kousouli D.C., CHt. All rights reserved. No part of this book may be reproduced or utilized in any form or by any means, electronic or mechanical including photocopying, recording, or by any information storage and retrieval system, without permission in writing from the author and publisher, except for the inclusion of brief quotations in a review with proper credit cited.

The BE A MASTER®BOOK SERIES (http://www.BEAMASTER.com) trademarked brand and work is Copyright of Dr. Theodoros Kousouli. The KOUSOULI® mark and the Kousouli® Method 4R Intervention health system are registered trademarks of Theodoros D. Kousouli D.C., CHt. and Kousouli Enterprises.

Heartfelt gratitude to the following for their contributions:

Editor: Penny Fletcher
Layout coordinator: Red Barn Muse Creative Group
Back cover headshot photography: Matthew A. Cooke
Cover image: Shutterstock; Gilmanshin

ISBN: 978-0-9989584-1-5 Softcover
ISBN: 978-0-9989584-2-2 Epub
ISBN: 978-0-9989584-3-9 Kindle

Kousouli Enterprises
P.O. Box 360494
Los Angeles, CA 90036

Printed in the United States of America

CONTENTS

Foreword vi

Disclaimers ix

Acknowledgements xi

Introduction xii

Chapter One: My Story - The Early Years 6

Chapter Two: History of Channeling Spirit 25

Chapter Three: Aligned in Synchronicity 33

Chapter Four: Learning from the Master 53

Chapter Five: Making Contact 58

Chapter Six: The Process of Channeling 68

Chapter Seven: Communicating Between Worlds 89

Chapter Eight: Wisdom from the Other Side 95

Conclusion 184

About the Author 185

Be A Master® Of Channeling Spirit

Life Changing Products · Books · Seminars · Empowerment Audios · Get on the Newsletter!
Connect with Dr. Kousouli, www.DrKousouli.com @DrKousouli #DrKousouli #KousouliMethod
You Will Also Enjoy Dr. Kousouli's Other Published Works. Available Now from Major Retailers:

BE A MASTER® OF MAXIMUM HEALING
How to Lead a Healthy Life Without Limits
- Holistic Solutions for over 60 Diseases to Help You and Your Loved Ones Heal!

BE A MASTER® OF PSYCHIC ENERGY
Your Key to Truly Mastering Your Personal Power
- Uncover and Amplify Your Hidden Psychic Abilities to Change Your Life!

BE A MASTER® OF SEX ENERGY
Hypnotize Your Partner for Love and Great Sex
- Build a Stronger Bond with Your Lover(s) Using Subconscious Science!

BE A MASTER® OF SUCCESS
Dr.Kousouli's 33 Master Secrets to Achieving Your Dreams
- Solid Success Principles You Can Apply Right Now to Empower Your Life!

BE A MASTER® OF SELF IMAGE
Dr.Kousouli's 33 Master Secrets to Living Healthier, Happier and Hotter
- Simple Holistic Tips & Tricks for More Weight Loss and Body Benefit to You!

BE A MASTER® OF SELF LOVE
Dr.Kousouli's 33 Master Secrets to Loving Your Extraordinary Life
- Overcome Bullying, Abuse, Depression and Build Massive Self-Esteem & Self-Love!

BE A MASTER® OF YOUR REALITY
Authentically Manifest Your Desires
- Use the Law of Attraction to Radically Transform Your Life!

If you would like to share your story of how Dr. Kousouli's books, audios or seminars have impacted your life for the better, we would love to hear from you!
For A Free Gift from Dr. Theo Kousouli visit www.FreeGiftFromDrTheo.com

This book is dedicated to the light workers who choose to live a life unrivaled - may your journey be immensely lit.

~

"He is most powerful who has power over himself."
~ Seneca

Foreword

"Each of us lives in multidimensions. We can choose where to focus our attention, and wherever that focus goes, a new reality opens up...through our attentions we bring these dimensions to life: We populate them, add new meaning, and paint unique pictures."
~ Deepak Chopra, *The Book of Secrets:*
Unlocking the Hidden Dimensions of Your Life

Channeling is a transpersonal and transcendent phenomenon. Contrary to the opinions of many, it is also a skill and an art. Therefore, it must be developed with care and dedication. Channeling development cannot be quantified or described as a formula. One thing is for sure; it is an expression of a unique 'relationship'. Truly, channeling is a relationship with an aspect of the Divine. We are all aspects of the Divine and so are those nonphysical consciousnesses with whom we can learn to communicate. These communications come from a nonlocal source that exists on some other level or dimension of reality other than the physical, as we know it.

Learning to channel, i.e. the 'channeling process' is an integrative, healing and personally transformational journey. It consists of steps and stages in which creative imagination, metaphor and imagery are consciously and creatively used to access other dimensions of reality and the self. Often this includes healing of one's inner child and inner adolescent aspects of one's self. Not always an easy task. Learning to attune to one's Higher Self becomes mandatory in order to become aware of the small self - or ego - that can block the receiving process.

With education and training channeled sources of wisdom, unseen friends, guides, and counselors, are able to communicate with us and enlighten our view of ourselves. Seeing reality through the lens of their worldview enables us to perceive ourselves as an integral part of Creation's unlimited interconnectedness.

Transcendent wisdom offers a worldview from 'outside the box' of the materialist view in which everything is created by matter and its laws. We can move beyond the 'the box' and instead see ourselves as creative consciousness choosing to manifest our lives and experiences. Recent studies of quantum physics point to how subatomic particles are affected by thought. The new science of quantum mechanics is based on the *primacy of consciousness*. This is the philosophy in which consciousness is the ground of all being, "…in which all material possibilities, including the brain, are embedded." (Amit Goswami, *Physics of the Soul*, p. 14)

Information received from channeled sources also has practical application in daily life. Unseen friends in spirit can help us understand how we can get in our own way of creating happiness in our lives.

Ultimately channeling is grounded in learning to receive Love with self-responsibility. Receiving unconditional Love from transpersonal realms is difficult if individuals are stuck in small-ego attitudes of victimhood or martyrhood. For over 30 years I've been blessed to teach channeling with Torah, the unseen consciousness I channel. It is only through healing the limited perspectives of one's self, inner child and inner adolescent that we grow. I have seen this first hand and am continually inspired by what I see: more acceptance of spiritual sources of communication as part of life itself. This phenomenon called channeling is now evolving our human consciousness more than ever before in our human history.

Dr. Theo Kousouli came to my classes eager, dedicated and ready to learn. Rarely have I seen such enthusiasm. He did 'the growth work' without reservation. In this book he candidly narrates his life's spiritual journey and process of opening to his own healing and channeling abilities. Spirit comes to him in the forms of several counselors, or guides.

Most notable is an ancient Greek wise-one called Heroditus. With focused intention and attention Theo carefully develops his relationship to Heroditus and other Unseen Friends. He seeks their counsel first on somewhat earthly scenarios bordering on needing to 'know the future'. However, he grows to ultimately understand, through his Spirit Counselors, Heroditus and Tony (another spirit source), that he must be self-responsible for co-creating his life from his free will. Heroditus and Tony open Theo to vast spiritual and human perspectives, which contribute to his self-empowerment, happiness and joy.

Rumi said, *"Come raise a joyful noise for we have found Friend, Beloved and Guide. What else is there in this world like this?"*

Theo offers the reader valuable information on the process of opening to channel vast insights for one's self. Those who learn to channel as Theo has done, learn to see themselves from a larger worldview of a meaning-filled purposeful life. And they come to *know* their own lovable, unlimited, boundless immortal nature.

We can all be grateful to Theo for sharing his remarkable journey...

Shawn Randall

Shawn Randall

Shawn Randall, M.A. is a trance channel, author, lecturer and teacher of metaphysics and channeling. She has extensively taught internationally in Japan, England and Mexico. Regarded by many as the number one channeling teacher in the country, her expertise and classes cover more than mental connectedness with spirit. She channels Torah, a wise and loving nonphysical being who facilitates energetic alignment with Unseen Friends thus allowing them to directly vocalize through their human channels. Shawn is a graduate of the University of Philosophical Research in Transformational Psychology. Shawn offers channeling courses at her Center for Personal Transformation in Los Angeles, California. Website: www.shawnrandall.com

Disclaimer

In a land where being politically correct seems more 'right' than standing for the 'truth,' or more desired than expressing an honest opinion, it's sad that I must digress and add the following legal disclaimer to remind you, the reader, that *you must think for yourself*.

This book is a collection of experiences and research that form my thoughts, opinions, and conclusions as a board-certified Doctor of Chiropractic (D.C.) and Hypnotherapist (CHt.); not a Doctor of Medicine (M.D.) or Psychiatrist. The content herein is controversial as it presents an alternate view to the status quo. There are establishments who may disagree with certain contents of this book and would have preferred that this information never found your eyes. However, this book is not intended for them; it was written for the countless individuals yearning for better health and well-being amongst a society that has lost its way.

The writings in this book are based on my personal research, experience, and interpretations. Your personal beliefs will affect your ability to review this material, as you will put it through your own filters. I intend to guide you in developing your own ability to use your personal energy in a healthy manner, and this book is a guide for you to grow but is not by any means the final word on the subject. I encourage you, the reader, to research, analyze, and develop your own opinions on the subject matters discussed. As a holistic health care provider, I express the truth as I have come to know it. It is my duty to aid in the growth of my beloved patients, family, and friends with this love so they too may reach the heights of what their Creator made possible for them to be.

Theodoros Kousouli D.C., CHt.

Be A Master® Of Channeling Spirit

Legal Disclaimer

This publication is for informational purposes only. The material presented herein denotes the views of the author as of the date of press. The material and ideas provided herein are believed to be truthful and complete, based on the author's best judgment and experience, formed from the available data at the time of publication. Because of the speed by which conditions and information change, the author reserves the right to amend and update his opinions at any time based upon the new data and circumstances. While every effort has been made to provide complete, accurate, current, and reliable information within this publication, no warranties of any kind are expressed or implied. The publisher, author, and all associated parties involved with this publication assume no responsibility for errors, inaccuracies, oversights, or conflicting interpretations of the content herein. The author and publisher do not accept any responsibility for any liabilities resulting from the use of this information. Readers acknowledge that the author is not engaging in rendering guarantees of income or outcome of any kind in connection with using any methods, techniques, tips, suggestions, or information stated or implied. Any perceived results of the material's use can vary greatly per case and individual circumstance. Mention of any persons or companies in this book does not imply that they endorse this book, its content, or the author, and similarly the author does not endorse them. Any supposed slights of specific establishments, corporations, organizations, peoples, or persons are unintended.

You should consult your own chiropractor, acupuncturist, herbalist, naturopath, hypnotherapist, or other holistic doctor(s) in combination with sound medical advice. Readers are cautioned to consult with proper health professionals about their individual circumstances on any matter relating to their health and personal well-being, prior to taking any course of action. The author is not a licensed medical doctor or psychiatrist and the *information provided in this book should not be construed as personal, medical, or psychiatric advice or instruction*. All readers or users of the information herein, who fail to consult proper health experts, assume the risk of any and all injuries.

The contents of this book and the information herein have not been evaluated or approved by the Food and Drug Administration for the treatment or cure of any disease, disorder, syndrome, or ailment mentioned herein.

Acknowledgements

"Thankfulness is the beginning of gratitude. Gratitude is the completion of thankfulness. Thankfulness may consist merely of words. Gratitude is shown in acts."
~ Henri Frederic Amiel

I would like to first thank my channeling instructor, Shawn Randall, who has helped me trust more and love deeper within myself, for the natural connection with my personal spirit guides to flourish.

My early mentors and colleagues in the healing arts, Dr. Scott Brown, Dr. Michael Kostas, Dr. Hari Bhajan Singh Khalsa, Dr. Scott Lewis, Dr. Elena Gabor, and my spiritual sister, intuitive medium Marisa Marinos for helping pave the path.

My mother for her unrelenting passion to keep my mind and heart focused on God. My father for his demonstration of work ethic and dedication to finishing what you start. My wonderful sister for sharing in this incredible journey with me and my brother for his continued love and support.

My life guides, angels and archangels who have been with me from the very beginning, blessing my path of spiritual evolution and providing total love. The feeling knowing you are there helping and loving me is just indescribable.

My editor Penny Fletcher and layout expert at Red Barn Muse Creative Group who were summoned by the powers described within this book to help the material find their form to you my reader.

Lastly, but definitely not least, I thank our Almighty Father Creator of all things visible and invisible, great and small, explainable and unexplainable. I stand in awe of your pure magnificence as you lead and sustain me through your playground day by day. IC-XC NI-KA. Amen.

This list deserves to be far longer than it reads. If I have forgotten your name in these writings of ink, kindly forgive me - and know that I am in gratitude to you from the depths of my heart.

Introduction

"Man: a being in search of meaning." ~ Plato

Countless life-changing experiences have shown me that ancient ways and new scientific studies can go hand in hand, although many modern physicians and scientists won't admit it. Ancient Eastern healing modalities are only now beginning to be commonplace in the United States, and most of the people who try them seem to want to find out more. Many of these practices are based on the body's own ability to heal. Do we Westerners, with all our modern medicines and techniques, throw out the baby with the bathwater when we ignore the knowledge of the ancients?

We all have so many gifts and talents we can explore together. My name is Dr. Theodoros Kousouli, and my gift is Intuitive Mind Body Holistic Healing. I'm based in Los Angeles, California, and I believe I have the unique ability to 'rewire' your nervous system into working optimally. After receiving my doctorate in healing through Chiropractic, I furthered my knowledge of hypnotherapy and mind-body healing by seeking exceptional mentors that grew my ability to understand my gift and what I was ultimately born to do with it. I have survived many challenges and adversities in my life and turned them from devastating calamities into positive and productive experiences that have blessed me with massive self-growth.

This book builds on my previous work, *BE A MASTER® of Psychic Energy*, where my readers learned about regaining control of their body's health and activating their psychic awareness through the Kousouli® Method by: **Re-**

moving toxins from the tissues, **Reviving** brain-body spinal connection, **Rebuilding** the body with proper nutrition and **Resetting** the internal programming and reconditioning of the conscious and subconscious mind, along with exploring extrasensory abilities, or what is commonly referred to as the sixth sense. Here, in *BE A MASTER® of Channeling Spirit,* we will continue these concepts with even more emphasis on deep inner connection to spirit through the **Resetting** aspect of our wiring in deeper understanding of the human and spirit connection. After all, we are not humans having a spiritual experience, we are spiritual beings having a human experience.

In addition to the *BE A MASTER®* book series, I offer one-on-one mind/body healing sessions, group seminars, private mentoring, hypnosis audios and home study courses. I'm excited to share my knowledge with you, so you may also experience and benefit from this type of healing as so many others have.

I have always been aware of a powerful presence with me and within me. As a child I remember many paranormal phenomena I couldn't explain to others at the time. I experienced lucid dreaming, visitations from unseen 'friends', and speaking to voices that made others accuse me of being 'alien'. Emotional pain from being misunderstood both within my family and in school, I circumvented almost committing suicide and chose instead to dive deep into the laws of the Universe to understand who I am and what I am doing on this Earth.

I learned to transform pain into joy and purpose, which furthered my healing. I learned how to love myself, became more compassionate, learned to control my empathy, while keeping my sense of humor and integrity.

Trying to explain my gift has been extremely challenging. My high school guidance counselor never prepared me for this! I have honed and developed this gift for more than twelve years during my early years in my Beverly Hills offices. Now, after finishing my latest book, I am reaching people all over the world and I can't explain how wonderful it feels to be able to bring such healing to others who previously had no hope. I am so humbled and grateful to all who have touched my life as they in effect helped me touch the world.

Why do you guide people through their health challenge(s)?

By trade, I am a spinal specialist; board certified as a doctor of chiropractic, a hypnotherapist with certification from the American Board of Hypnotherapy and I hold a certification in medical musculoskeletal ultrasonography. However, what I fully do as a healer, has no clear definition yet as I am pioneering this type of work. I further my personal experience with esoteric sciences and knowledge of the mind through metaphysical research and teachings daily. Because I had such a hard time understanding my gifts (with no support) as a child as I mentioned earlier, and being born with a faulty heart valve, my journey on this earth has definitely been one described best as a school of 'Hard Knocks'. I was semi-paralyzed from a pool accident in my late teens and received chiropractic care to recover fully from it when doctors had prescribed drugs and surgery as my only options. I then recovered rapidly from major open-heart surgery to replace my aortic heart valve at age 28. I had that same valve replaced again (along with my aortic arch, the tube above the heart that sends blood to my body) at 39 and healed even faster in just two months' time using the techniques I have developed and written about in my books, available now online, worldwide. I feel that my life's experiences both as a medical patient and as a holistic health practitioner in the wellness paradigm for more than twelve years, offers those who seek me the best chance at success for understanding and attaining their health and well-being. Think of me as a super specialist of your nervous system and lifestyle. I find what is not serving you and I help you correct it. TOGETHER, we both work towards a better, stronger version of you.

What is your gift and how do you explain your work?

I am an intuitive empath and can feel and direct subtle energy (chi or 'pneuma') through healing. An empath is a person who has high sensory awareness, or sixth sense, capable of feeling the emotions or physical symptoms of others even if they themselves are not going through the same situation or events. Empaths are very in-tune with their surroundings. For this reason, I do not spend much time in disruptive crowds as this can be draining to the auric field. The emotional abuse as a child I referred to earlier caused me to shut down my inborn sensitivity because I wanted to conform or 'fit in' with others and not be branded as 'different'. This dormant ability however reemerged after my first open heart surgery and unlocked the extra-sensory abilities which have become even keener since my second heart surgery. I have struggled all my life with understanding the process and coming to terms with this 'gift'. Not until recent years did I come to terms with, or even understand what my name means. My full birth name is Theodoros Demosthenis Kousouli which broken down means: *Theo (Greek for God) Doro (Greek for Gift) Demostheneis (Greek for messenger and orator of/for the people; populace) Kous (From 'Kusur' Turkish slang for scar or blemish) Souli (soul or a city in Greece, Souli) or God's Gift for the peoples' scared souls.* Ironically, I have a large scar on my chest from my two heart surgeries and my life is dedicated to helping patients heal their lives on a very deep neural, emotional, physical and spiritual level. I appropriately developed my abilities and knowledge into the Kousouli® Method and this is what patients say changes their lives so rapidly. My training as a chiropractor and hypnotherapist was the basis for my technical training, however I do not need any of my technical training to do what I do but rather rely on my intuitive mind. During sessions with my clients I see, and feel their subtle energy; in other words, their auras. I receive mental images from their chakras and bio field which directs me to administer specific care at that exact moment. At times their spirit will give information that comes through and I relay it verbally to them if it is fitting for their life's journey. It tends to very much vibrate with the patient's needs and often may take some time to sink in before they understand the information's significance. Every session can seem similar but is in many ways different. In some sessions I touch the patient's spine or interact with their auric energy; other times I don't. It is a case by case basis unique to the patient's journey.

Why do people specifically seek you out?

Many in the U.S. look like the 'walking dead' living a life that's not authentically the person they are intended to be. It's a condition I call 'Spiritual anorexia'. They have struggled to attain the cars, the money, the titles, and the fame but they have lost the joy of spirit. This shows up as dysfunction in their lives, and primarily as health problems. Often, they see many other doctors and then - they find my door. However, I couldn't help people if I myself haven't been through the path to learn to heal myself from these same spiritual, mental, emotional, and physical afflictions (which you will soon read about).

Many people come see me because of a physical ailment that is bothering them, such as a neck, low back, shoulder, etc. This is what may bring them in for care but that is the end 'malfunction' portion of their pain process. They soon see that their physical ailment was brought forth from things they were chronically thinking of, or their body was feeling, but did not pay attention to it. Now their body sounds the alarm and they find me to give them the message and guidance on how to reverse their disease process. If you don't pay attention to your nonphysical esoteric alerts, you will eventually get a physical alert (or dis-ease) to wake you up.

Not for the Cynical

Our world is quickly transforming itself now more than ever before. As individuals change themselves, so does mass consciousness. I believe my ability to serve as I do meets the demands of mass consciousness. We are all energy and our thoughts mold this energy. I feel and sense the energy through working with a person's bio-field. If you know how to influence belief systems and are able to imprint them correctly into one's mind and body, you can 'theoretically' change dimensions and time. Scientists believe if you change something in the loop of time, you re-write the future and the past may have never occurred. In other words, the events of life that repeat will be nullified and new possibilities can emerge. We are coming to understand that everything esoteric, even if not yet fully understood, may be rooted also in a scientific basis. Our traditional Eastern and Western therapies are recombining with ancient wisdom while major new discoveries are being made.

Science has been excellent in explaining what is already understood in a linear 3-D accepted thought process. Scientists try their best at using understood principles to explain the still unexplainable. Science is however poor at explaining what it is ignorant about. And there will come a time in the not-so-distant-future where it will finally understand and be able to explain God. We can see that quantum physics is helping 'science' in some way deal with the idea of Creationism. It is difficult to put a multidimensional idea such as the power of God and Spirit in terms the limited linear human mind can understand. Through our frustrations however, we do try. I do not write this book for cynical doubters who wish to keep a closed mind. If it is your wish to hold onto a closed-minded perspective, that is your right to do so. However, I do invite those who have a healthy skepticism and are willing to look past their current rigid mental system for more understanding and further life expression. For myself, I have tested my limited beliefs and present my own experiences so that others who look beyond the limited can also open their hearts to the power that created them. If you, the reader, need more researched solid proof before you can accept that any of what is written in these pages can occur, there are many books from a medical perspective to help you understand scientifically the reality of life after death and the continuation of communication between universal dimensions and realities. Read *Surviving Death; A Journalist Investigates Evidence of Afterlife* by Leslie Kean and *Home at the Tree of Life* by Dr. Elena Gabor.

Chapter One: My Story – The Early Years

"Know thyself" ~ Socrates

I had the best of two dogmatic worlds; a military father and a very religious mother. I grew up in a Greek American Eastern Orthodox home, in a very traditional setting, consisting of the rare 'nuclear' family, with my wonderful two younger siblings who are fraternal twins. My father, a strict former Merchant Marine for the Greek Navy, became a restaurant owner when he emigrated to the United States in the 1970s, whereas my mother was a traditional stay-at-home mom who took care of three highly energetic kids. She was, and still is, a very religious woman, devoted to the Greek Orthodox Church's teachings, which resulted in my two siblings and I being raised in the ways of the church.

We lived in Deptford, New Jersey, in a quiet middle-income suburban town barely on the map. My father always provided the tough love, practical work ethic, food, clothing, and roof over our heads. My mother provided the religious education needed to live a structured life within society.

As a young woman she became interested in a nun who was performing miraculous healings in Greece. She met this woman through a friend who went to a monastery near her home town. After my mother lost her first child as a stillborn, she was anxious to get some divine words of encouragement that her (then) 3-month-old baby - me - was going to be okay in his development. This woman gave my mother an interesting message in a hand-written letter that read like this: "God has heard your prayer. I had a vision of blessing you and your husband. As I laid the cross on your forehead and then the forehead of your husband, there was a blinding bright light and I heard a loud voice say, "The boy will grow up to be a very prosperous and great man."

For a Long Time, that Didn't Seem True Because I Just Didn't Fit In

I remember being a joyful, nerdy little child who loved everyone. I would go up to people and hug and kiss them on the cheek without second-guessing my actions. I was full of love, and thoughts of anger, hate, jealousy, and other negative emotions were not in my nature or vocabulary. My mother could not stop my impulsiveness and would sternly reprimand me that it was not good to kiss strangers, even on the cheek. I asked, "But why Mom?" and she laughingly said, "It is just not what you do." I again asked, "But why Mom? I love them." I remember her face as she smiled and slowed down to explain it in terms my ten-year-old mind would understand. "Big Boy (the nickname I earned since I was the oldest of three), you can hug them or shake their hand but no more kissing OK?" I was puzzled and sad about that, but I obeyed my mother and fell into line like everyone else in society, as I shook hands and remained socially acceptable.

Between the ages of four and twelve, I believe I had extra sensory abilities; one of them being that I could fly. Later in life I found out that while asleep, I was experiencing a phenomenon called astral traveling, where your soul vividly explores the wonders of all Creation. A feeling of lifting and flying is common with this phenomenon as you cannot tell the difference between the physical world and the astral world. I seriously felt as if this was an ability I could do without hesitation and was confident it was possible for me to do any time I wished. I told my mother and father about this, and they kept telling me it was a dream and that it would go away. I never questioned it. However, to my disappointment and frustration, it became less frequent, happening only 50-percent of the time. As I got older, it did not happen much past 14 years of age. Because I thought everyone knew about this ability I was confused and wanted to get answers from my parents. But "Leave me alone, I'm watching the news," or, "Get out of the way, I can't see the T.V.," was a common response from my father when I tried to share my thoughts or concerns.

In the Beginning, School Was Just as Strange for Me

I never liked public school. It reminded me of a prison system, where the principal was the warden and the teachers controlled the classrooms and patrolled the hallways; always on the lookout for escapees. I felt confined behind the brick walls of the compound and felt that no matter how hard I tried, I could not do well enough to meet teacher expectations, nor be cool enough to avoid the bullies on the recess fields. In my grade school years, I was perceived as a tiny, odd, and quiet kid. I was the smallest person in the class, often bullied for nothing more than looking like an easy target for others to release their day-to-day insecurities and stress upon. However, deep down inside myself I felt like a giant, multitalented genius and more powerful than a king. I felt this way throughout my childhood, though the feeling was suppressed daily by negative people in my immediate environment.

In those years, the school system didn't fully challenge us, nor did it encourage identifying and growing our individual innate abilities. Instead, school would be the same mundane cycle day in and day out; and as long as you did not think for yourself and stayed subordinate, you got a good grade. I never felt school was about actual learning, just rote memorization and regurgitating it back in time for the test, only to forget the material and never use most of it again. The bell would ring, we would have to switch books, and report to the next class like good little prisoners. I detested the system for not tapping into my more profound abilities, or, recognizing that I was someone who had more than just rote memorization to offer the world. I wanted to be free to create and express myself without repression. Being the oldest of the siblings in our household, I was by nature a very rebellious free thinker with high energy. I excelled without effort in courses such as English, Science, Art, and Music, but I did not take well to authoritative suppression of my childhood freedoms and liberties. Plus, I always felt I was different from my classmates. Obviously, some of them felt I was too, which resulted in bullying.

In an Instant, I Learned the Environment Was Sick, Not Me!

On the refrigerator door in our kitchen there was a photo my mother particularly liked of us as kids. But my sister would tease me about how I looked in it, "Look at your pointed ears, you're an alien, you're an alien! Theo's adopted from another planet!" to which I replied, "I am not an alien, I am not adopted, and I am not from another planet." I would get really upset, because I wanted to fit in so badly. In many ways, however, I did feel very alien. By the time I was 15, the bullying at school was overwhelming. Tormented by bullies in class, unable to decipher the dreams and visions, and the emotional abuse at home, I became convinced that I was too crazy and too different to fit in.

One day after school, beat up and emotionally lifeless, drowning in tears, I'd decided to end my life by cutting my wrists with a razor. Just as I was about to slice my wrists, a voice inside sternly said, "NO!" It echoed so loudly it vibrated through me like lightning and I couldn't bring myself to take the razor across my wrists; my grip on the razor went limp. An overwhelming peace and calm came over me, as I felt comforted by a feeling unlike any other. I somehow internally understood at that moment that I was not meant to end my life and that it was the environment that was sick, not me. I knew I was here for a reason and believed there was something grander that I needed to do in the future. I knew not where this instant clarity came from, but it was very much welcomed and saved my life. Soon after that event, a strong boost in confidence came when my English teacher walked up to me after I read out loud for the class. She paused, leaned in and said to me, "Theodore, your beautiful voice one day will be heard by millions."

As I grew through my youth and teens, my classmates and siblings would ask me, "Why are you talking to yourself?" They'd laugh and tease me, wiggling their lips and making funny faces. What was really going on was that I was talking to someone, sometimes a Guide, or perhaps God or some other higher power. I would see colors vividly and I felt as if I was multitasking in two worlds. As mumbling would occur, sounds and thoughts would often come in a very fast manner. I hardly noticed it happening as I was in a dialogue in my brain, in what seemed like a daydream state, though still conscious about the happenings in the world around me. My sister would tease me and say, "Mom, Theo's talking to himself again!" I would pretend to laugh and hide it by making a joke, so as to not to humiliate myself trying to explain what was really going on and provoke more bullying.

Fortunately, Despite the Misunderstandings, the Visions Continued

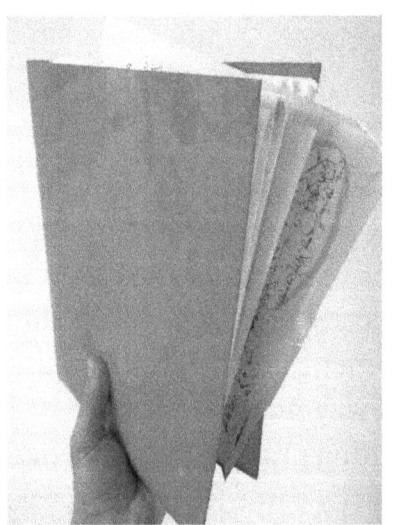

After my mother gave me a copy of the letter from the Greek nun mentioned earlier in this chapter, on my 13th birthday, she told me her backstory and what the letter meant. As a typical teenager I could care less and never gave this any thought again until I entered college and a girl I liked asked me what my astrological sign was and if I knew that astrology and numerology held truths about my personality and my life. "The baby Jesus was found using astrology," she said. And there was no doubt, she was right. So, this peaked my interest and I started collecting anything about my life I could, including anything told to me by seers, readers or 'psychics'. I saved it all and filled up a folder to accompany the letter my mother gave me. This folder contains all the 'data' I have accumulated on who the stars and psychic seers told me I am. My mission was to understand who I was and to strengthen my faith in what I believed in, because at the time I only had information about who I thought I was. If an outside source could verify what I felt internally, I may understand better my life, myself, and my purpose. To a young man who was lost and looking to find his path, this was very attractive to me. Throughout my young adulthood, there would be both good and bad experiences that frustrated my understanding and beliefs of the outwardly unseen world. But as a child I remember many vibrant images during dream states and also did astral traveling nightly.

For example, of one of these experiences, at the age of thirteen, I recall being in my room at my desk doing homework and blacking out into a vision of a man in a uniform touching someone lying lifeless on a table. I saw people crowded in a grey room overlooking the body on the table. The man who sat at the top end of the table touched the still body's neck, releasing a bright light (resembling the blue flame that comes from electricity), which then flowed down the body and around the table lighting the whole room. Instantaneously, the body became animated and I awakened out of the vision. When I came back, my hands were pulsing, sweating, and very warm. I was in shock from what had just occurred. I was waving my hands as you would if you just realized you had touched a hot stove and were fanning them out to cool them down. However, I soon realized that I was all right and my hands were not burned. I immediately left my paperwork and ran downstairs, flew out the door and went three houses down to my younger brother and sister who were at our friend Kelsie's house (our usual hangout after school where we would go to escape boredom). Out of breath and still high from excitement, I started huffing and puffing as I ran up to my brother and sister who were on the backyard swing set. Looking at my hands I said, "Something happened, there was a blue light!" I blurted out in a squeaky huff-and-puff voice. "What? You're crazy," said my sister, followed by the laughter of my brother and Kelsie. I started to clam up to avoid further humiliation and decided it would be best just to leave. Between the bullying in school for being different, and the lack of support from my own family, I crawled inside myself - deep inside.

I continued having dreams, even seeing what I believe was an angel resembling the Virgin Mary, looking and smiling at me while sitting at the table with my mother and sister one morning. My mother was the only one who would even entertain the possibility of me seeing anything like that. Mothers are inherently powerful psychics by nature; the protective instinct for their children is often aided by their sixth sense. Throughout my life, my mother was the most supportive when I reported sightings and had dreams, as she herself was used to her own events of dream premonitions and psychic phenomenon.

Incidental Blessings

One summer break, we went to Greece to visit our grandmother. During our stay, we visited a summer camp for teens to get out of Athens which was always very busy. Getting a little mountain air is what my mother thought would be best, since it allowed us (American children) to make some Greek friends at the camp and enjoy our summer a little more.

Boys will be boys, and we played games of "Chicken" as we wrestled in the pool to see who would be victorious. That's where two people would hoist a person on their shoulders and see who could knock the other pair down first. In a round that did not go our way, my partner on my shoulders lost the wrestling match and as he fell, his legs took my head and neck with him. There was a violent turn to the right, and I felt an immediate sharp searing pain deep in my neck and chest. It felt as if someone had lodged a dagger deep into me. My left arm felt limp as I gave all my effort to move it, and I was suddenly having difficulty breathing. There were no positions I could move to escape the pain, and even swallowing was a difficult task. My heart and lungs slowed down, labored in their function, as if someone had hit the slow-motion button. It was frightening to feel that way; so vulnerable, fragile, as if I could die at any moment. At the same time, any head movement made me feel as if hot liquid tar was running down my neck, back, and chest; even at the slightest quiver of motion. After I was pulled out of the pool, I calmed down. My condition stabilized slightly but could hardly be called 'improved' during our remaining time in Greece, until we headed back to the States to get proper care. My mother did all she could to comfort me and told me it would get better, although even she felt helpless to offer any thoughts on how. My father, being ex-military, told me to bear the pain, and even teased me about it; telling me to just, "tough it out like a Spartan". It could've been easy for anyone to give such advice, since I looked perfectly normal on the outside, but I felt like I was dying slowly on the inside. My mother's voice of reason pressured my father to take me to our family medical doctor. My father routinely looked at the overall expenses and costs of a medical visit rather than its benefits, but after weighing the options of not having to hear me whine anymore from the pain, he reluctantly took me to get checked. The doctor took my medical history, X-rays, did a small evaluation and then brushed it off as a strain-sprain of the neck. I received a prescription for painkillers from the M.D., and he told us the pain would soon go away.

A little ice, pain pills, and rest, then my problems would be a thing of the past, right? Wrong! Two weeks later I felt the same pain without any relief. On the follow-up visit, the doctor suggested an MRI, with the possibility of surgery if nothing else worked. They were not the options any of us wanted to entertain, and my father cringed at the $2,000-plus costs which was what an MRI cost back then, so we waited it out to see if my pain would at least lessen in severity by the next week. When the 'kink' in my neck didn't improve much, I slowly managed to drive myself to a massage therapist for a treatment. With clenched teeth, I held back screams of pain as the masseuse pushed on my neck trying to relieve the knot. Next, I found myself in a physical therapist's office, but the pain made that also impossible to get any treatment done properly; hindered by all my moaning and pain, as I felt worsening irritation with every movement. After many sleepless nights and many tears shed, one day I passed by a local chiropractor's office. The office was busy and there were many cars outside, but from the things my father had said about chiropractors I was afraid to even try walking through the door. My father felt chiropractors were not to be trusted, with their 'pseudo-science' back-and-neck-popping wrestling maneuvers. He said we would just be wasting more money. Of course, as with most things misunderstood, my father spoke about what he heard from rumors and mass media, not from what he'd experienced with a chiropractor for himself. Yet, thoughts of voodoo, chanting, lotions and potions ran through my mind when I heard the word chiropractor (thanks to my father) and also because of my own lack of understanding and research at that time.

I figured since nothing else had worked to cure my arm, chest pain, and semi-paralysis, maybe some voodoo magic would bring me relief. I was ready to try anything! Somehow, I convinced my father to take me to the chiropractor. I remember that day clearly, as I lay down on the table staring at the light on the ceiling, waiting to be seen. I was motionless and hopeful, but mostly fearful. When the doctor came into the room he looked nothing like the witch doctor I had envisioned in my mind, but was a very professional, youthful, energetic gentleman in his early 40's who seemed very confident that he could help my condition from what he saw on my X-rays. I'd gone to specialists within the medical field who looked much more knowledgeable and were also much older than this guy, but he was telling me he was sure he could fix me up. I relaxed the best I could, but my doubt turned to fear again as he took hold of my head, felt my neck muscles, and pushed to feel the specific bone alignment he'd viewed on the X-rays. He instructed me to breathe and I found my thoughts wandering as I closed my eyes. "God please don't let him further paralyze or kill me," I remember saying to myself. Others had tried to move my neck and nothing good came out of it other than more pain and moaning. Then, just as I ended my pleading thoughts, in one fast effortless swoop of his hands and tilt of my neck, I heard an audible noise and a current of power surged into my body. I started to gasp at what felt like ten thousand waterfalls overtaking me in a rush of relief. I had such a moment of peaceful serenity from the sudden release of pain that I was now in tears, lying on my back in this voodoo witch doctor's room, totally amazed at what had taken place in just a fraction of a second. My arm started to tingle and re-animate as my heart and lungs were going back to full speed and regulating. A great deal of the pain lifted, and I was speechless and in awe of every feeling I was having! My life force was coming back; it was once again flowing through me and being expressed with vitality. Still speechless and with my mouth wide open, I sat up and started moving again. What a miracle! I remember wiping back tears as I asked the doctor, "What happened? What did you do to me? What did you do differently that no one else could do? What are you? You cured me! I can't understand why I didn't come here first!" I had so many questions. He said, "I removed the interference (subluxation) from your neck, and your brain was able to reconnect again to your body through your nervous system, allowing the full expression of your life to flow again." With total amazement, wonder, respect and gratitude I uttered the words that began everything I am today: "I want to do this for others, just like you did it for me. I want to free people like you freed me!" Soon after that I registered for school to learn the healing manual therapeutic art and science that is called CHIROPRACTIC (Greek "Chiro," meaning "hand"; "Praktikos," meaning "done by/practiced by").

When I told my father how life-changing the experience was and that I now wanted to be a chiropractor, my father could not understand how much I valued the work I had seen with my own eyes and experienced first-hand. He even feared the shame my decision to go into chiropractic might bring upon the family. His limited knowledge of what chiropractic healing really was (and is) over-rode what this science and art could do, as the public did not recognize it as widely then as it does today.

Finally, I Left Home and Began to Make Sense of My Life

Going to college meant I was able to leave my small town long enough to mix my mind with more seasoned, interesting people. Like all young men and women moving along toward adulthood, I questioned many times on what scholastic concentration to focus, and what career path to take. I knew I wanted to decide on a pre-medical major and entertained the idea of a general medical family practice, dentistry, podiatry, or dermatology. If not the medical option, then it would be either an engineer or politician; my father's choices for me – not mine.

Thanks to our religious mother, some form of spirituality had always been alive in our household. Throughout the years I would pray at night before bed, and I remember asking God to help me find work I could do that would help others and provide me peace of mind, so I would enjoy my life. I was confused with who I was, or if I had a purpose, and questioned why I even existed. I asked God to make the answer very clear for me, so I would know without a doubt what He wanted me to do with this life. I witnessed how difficult my father's life was as he slaved in the restaurant business to provide for us yet came home and hardly had any time to spend with us as a family. I really think he wanted to enjoy his life with us, but there was no more energy in him after the long 12-hour shifts he endured. From a young age I could see that this was not healthy. The stress from slacking employees, rude customers, and day-to-day operations was unfortunately taken out on my mother, siblings, and I whenever he did have the time to spend with us. I was more interested in going into life utilizing my talents as an artist; making large projects and sculptures for museums, collectors, and art galleries. However, I always had a fondness for the magnificent work of art that the human body is, and its workings continue to leave me in awe every day. Little to my understanding at that time, God was soon about to put my life together for me in ways that helped it all make sense.

Yes, college and the years that followed were a new beginning for me.

Fast Forward to Age 28: Valuable Lessons in Health - Round 2

October 5, 2005. I will never forget that day. I remember it vividly, as anyone in my position would. *"You have about eight months to live if we don't get your aortic valve replaced. Your heart will give out and then you'll internally bleed to death."*

It does not sink in - at first - when you're told you might die soon. Time speeds up, as if racing you to see if you can catch up.

Life was stressful with relationships, board exams, and mounting bills. After passing out at my desk twice within a week for no reason, I got concerned and got full blood work, a physical, EKG's, and echocardiograms to find out why I was blacking out. Up until then, when I felt any chest pains, I had the typical macho tough-guy mentality: Stick it out as long as possible and deny everything, even if it kills you. Thank God common sense prevailed because I worried that I might black out while driving and submitted to more tests and follow-up visits. It was just like the movies - I would be fully alert and then suddenly, it was as if someone had turned the lights out; only this time there was no beautiful vision or premonition like I'd had in my teens. How ironic that my mother had always told me I had a big heart; *literally, I did!* The cardiologist called it cardiomegaly: a condition of an enlarged heart caused by the stress of pumping blood out to the body. My aortic valve was malformed since birth with two cusps (bicuspid) instead of the normal three (tricuspid). Instead of pumping blood away from my heart towards my head and neck where it should have traveled, my aortic valve's two leaflets had become over-stressed, and were leaking blood (regurgitating it) backwards towards the heart. As a result, I blacked out because of the lack of oxygen and nutrients to my brain.

Terror once again gripped me as I remembered the swimming pool accident years earlier. My fears worsened as I inherently wondered if the heart murmur that I was diagnosed with as a child had suddenly suffered enough stress. Now that innocent little heart murmur I was born with, that gave me three heartbeats instead of two, was about to go on permanent strike. I was still too young for my heart to be taking a final lap around the track, when I had not done all the things in life I wanted to do. You can say that my "lack of" life started to flash before my eyes, as I began to see my uncertain future, and all the things I'd said I would get to later. "Later" was suddenly sooner than anyone could have expected - especially to 28-year-old me!

As I stared at the clock wishing the second hand would not move so fast, I began to resent myself for not traveling more, wasting away days, not saying "I love you" more to my family, and not spending enough quality time with friends. As my lack of life became crystal clear, I wasn't happy with what I saw.

I was at my cardiologist's office for my final appointment before scheduling my surgery, and I argued with the doctor. "But there has to be another way to fix it without having to be on Coumadin for the rest of my life. That's like a death sentence!" I raged on: "It's like rat poison. That stuff is a slow death. In addition, I'd have to monitor my blood levels every day? No…no way. Not me. How can this be modern medicine? Hasn't something more progressive been invented by now?"

I was upset that the only options I had were a metal valve that needed Coumadin (blood thinners to keep the metal joints of the valve from clotting with possibilities of stroke), or an animal valve that would eventually fail and then need to be replaced with another surgery in the future. I had two not-so-fabulous choices but was grateful I still had choices that could keep me alive. I chose the natural cow-bovine valve, even knowing it would only be a matter of time that I might be going through the same fate again in the future, when the valve degenerated. However, unlike the metal valve's need for blood thinners, with a natural cow's valve I would have a chance at a more normal life.

I was snarling at the doctor for not having better solutions and felt angry with God that I was in this position. I felt there had to be another way. The cardiologist tried to calm me down, stoically touching my shoulder, but his forehead was wrinkled with worry.

After many exhausting nights of deep thought, I finally made peace with the fact I had to go through with the surgery. Before I knew it, the surgery date came, and I was prepped and put into my requisite gown. I kissed my family goodbye and watched them disappear into the waiting room, as my mortality was becoming clearer by the second. "*I may never see them again,*" I thought to myself as I was wheeled down the cold hospital hallway to the operating room for what seemed like forever. I quietly started to pray. In desperation and mounting anger, I was beginning to lose my faith, but like most folks facing possible death, I decided to make a deal with God.

I realized that I'd lived too selfishly and egotistically up to this point in my life. I took too much for granted - my family, my friends, my time, my purpose - my whole life. What a waste it would be to let this life go without making something more of the gifts and talents I'd been given. I remember praying, *"God If you want me to come back - And yes I do want to come back - I will dedicate my time to serving you through helping others. Let me know you are with me when I ask, and when people ask for help, let me be able to give it to them through your grace. But please, if you want me to open my eyes and come back to continue this life, please make it easier for me so that I don't have to struggle like I used to. God, I want to feel love. I want to know what love is - Real Love. If you agree to all this, then I want to live and fulfill the highest purpose you have for me here."* With those last words in my mind, I saw the anesthesiologist's hand place the mask over my face as I dropped into rest. I had finally let go and surrendered myself, and as I did so, I allowed my soul much needed inner peace.

The surgery was rough; the surgeon had to open me up again a second time after they believed they were done. I bled internally, and they raced to re-stabilize me. My folks in the waiting room were very worried, and my mother went into super-prayer mode. The surgeon's second attempt, although completed later than planned, was a success. As I came in and out of consciousness, I could see things coming into focus. I was on machines, unable to breathe for myself, and in a strange bed with tubes everywhere. I saw what looked like a white lab coat come into focus. Then I saw a doctor or technician in front of me doing his routine business. I made noises of distress and finally caught his attention; he turned to me, saw I was awake, flipped a few switches, and I was able to breathe again. I frantically took many deep breaths, and I was out again - back to a deep sleep. It was such a freaky moment. It was what I now remember as my second chance – my rebirth in the Intensive Care Unit.

Post ICU, nurses used me as a human pincushion as they jabbed both my arms for blood every few hours. They missed my highly-visible veins several times, to the point that I angrily yelled at the staff and said I would endure no more blood withdrawals. I would listen to the small talk of nurses as they came into my room during their routine checks, and I could tell who truly had their heart in their work and who was there just to pass the shift. The unappetizing processed meals including wheat, milk, and cheese products given to patients were too unhealthy for recovery or proper body nutrition. The television helped stimulate our brains, but they had it on negative news castings. I would get myself out of bed and take walks around the hospital since there was no rehab program that encouraged body movement or stretching there. As I passed others' rooms in the hallway and peeked in, I would witness people in agony and with a stoic trance of desperation evident in their eyes, some would stare at me while lying motionless in their hospital beds. I had an eerie feeling that it didn't matter to the staff If I got better or if they kept me there as long as possible; there was no actual push or healthy incentive to get better soon after surgery. It seemed to be their job just to monitor me. I started realizing how hospitals were a big business; with many holding cells for the sick, each of which made the hospital a profit. Post-surgery, the majority of my real healing was to happen outside those walls, not within them. As I came to the conclusion that only I could get myself back to 100-percent from where I was at that moment, I asked to be released as soon as possible and decided to take recovery into my own hands.

In subsequent visits, the cardiologist told me that full recovery would take four-to-six months. I was impatient and wanted to get on with my new life; there was too much to do. I always knew from my hypnosis and mind-body studies how powerful suggestions were, and that the mind can speed up recovery. I went into meditation every chance I got while in the hospital and after being released. I must have meditated for 14 hours a day. I would envision my cells healthy, my heart repairing itself and reinforcing tissues around the new valve. I would see myself in the gym, running, in the pool swimming, jumping rope, and doing other activities; trying always to see myself as normal, healthy, and free. I was alive, my heart was beating, and I was amazed at what I'd just experienced. A cow's valve was now functioning as my heart valve! I was extremely grateful for my surgeon's knowledge and skill.

Back home, I enjoyed my mom's fine Greek cooking, took my vitamins, supplements, herbs, drank plenty of fluids, watched many funny movies, and only discussed positive things with positive people. I neglected to take my pain meds though; I didn't like how they slowed down my digestive system, giving me horrid constipation and unbearable pain in my abdomen. I focused on the benefits of not taking the pills because I knew from my chiropractic studies how painkillers and other drug neurotoxins can affect the nervous system, prohibiting healing instead of aiding it. With constant meditation, my mind quickly dealt with the pain as if I had taken the painkillers. When I gained the strength to get around, I immediately scheduled a treatment with the same "voodoo" chiropractor who had healed me from semi-paralysis years earlier. The trauma of the operation and bad positioning in the hospital bed had my neck and body misaligned. Now that the surgeon had done his amazing job of replacing the valve, it was my job to give my body what it needed to recover. I knew when the chiropractor properly adjusted my neck it would take away all internal neurological stress, and I would start to heal much more quickly, as my body's energy would focus completely on the heart again. Since the neck is the pathway to the rest of the body (especially the chest, heart and lungs), this would open vital pathways and my brain could begin fixing and sending proper nutrients to their respective places for repair without hindrance. The combination of good nutrition, meditation, rest, visualization, self-hypnosis, a loving environment, and chiropractic care allowed me to super heal completely in about 45 days post-surgery!

I remember finishing a bench-press set upon returning to the gym in awe and gratitude to God that I was able to get back to life so quickly after such a major surgery. The steps I took post-op helped heal my heart so that I could quickly resume living with purpose.

After I Was Healed, I Went into Practice to Heal Others

After I started my practice, I found that when I placed my hands-on people's bodies I would receive visions of their life that played like movies in my mind's eye. This started me looking into my unseen abilities and when I finally built up the nerve to tell a patient about what I was seeing, they would exclaim, "how did you know that?" To my amazement, what I was seeing were then verified as real events that were the root of the pain or issue they were experiencing. The visions were starting to be overwhelming and I needed to make sense of them, so I sought out teachers on the subject and started taking meditation and clairvoyant classes.

On my first reading encounter with my instructor in clairvoyance, she said, "First we must read you; the whole class will read your aura, chakras and energy. Before you become a student of clairvoyant work you must experience a reading yourself." I was excited and ready to go through the process for myself. During the reading I tested the teacher, "Of all the lives my spirit has lived as a human, I am curious to know, what was the happiest life I lived?" A few moments later, she said, "You're showing me a life as a monk or priest, you are wearing a robe with belt tassels, not like current robes a priest wears, more of a brownish faded robe. The timing is a castle-like era, seems cloudy, very foggy type of weather - Ireland or Britain. You are very happy, content as it seems, you do not have much, but life is enjoyed by the simpler things." I heard many amazing things that night, including how the interactions of my life and between my parents clicked. But the monk lifetime vision stuck with me.

About a month later, I was doing computer research on esoteric topics when I came across a YouTube video of a Texas woman who claimed she could read Akashic records - the records of our past lives that are stored within our DNA. Well that was 'way out there' and naturally my curiosity peaked. I said no way can that happen. I'll call her and waste $165 in the name of research by getting a reading. This was an extraordinary claim and I had to cross-check this with what my teacher told me in my past life session. With a snarky smile on my lips I called her and went right for the big question, "Which of my past lives was I the happiest in?" A few minutes of silence passed, and her voice came back with, "You were a monk, in Ireland, during the difficult times of the plague. You were grateful to just be alive and served those who came to the monastery for soup in the kitchens there. People came from all over not just for the food, but the kindness, hope and words you gave each of them. You fed not just their body but their soul as well." Now the silence was coming from my side of the phone. I had practically fallen out of my chair. She continued, "You also had a great voice and would also sing to them, it gave them great comfort." The reading continued, and it was also amazing with intimate truths no one could know, only me. My brain then was at a major crossroad. How can two women, who are unrelated, and do not know each other, are in different states - one in California and the other in Texas, who have no idea who I am, and at totally different times give me the exact same answer as to what my happiest past life was? And with so much detail? And details that parallel my life's work today? I am very much happy to be alive considering my heart surgeries and previous traumas, and I do tend to the masses both physically and emotionally through my profession. I have recorded songs and taken singing lessons, as I loved to sing since I was a child. I also soothe people vocally through hypnotherapy and my audio sessions. All are very much applicable to my life now as then. Neither of the two psychic readers knew who I was, they only knew my first name when I told them at the reading it was Theo. So, it was evident to me that something I was carrying in my aura, DNA, or energy field was able to be read or 'picked up' by those who are sensitive enough to make sense of this information. My mind was blown, and I didn't look back, I knew this was real, and I wanted to know everything about it. And that *everything* is much of what I have written in my books.

Over the years, I have dug deep with the help of many wonderful healers, seers and readers and received valuable information that has shown me truths and clues that led to my current life. Through regression hypnosis I have relived past lives as King Solomon, a Roman soldier, an American Indian herbal healer, a lawyer in 1800's in the United Kingdom, a widow on a farm with eight children, a monk in Ireland, a Greek sculptor, a Greek healer in war camps, a servant to a vile king in the Middle ages, an African American slave in the south, and many other adventures; each holding a piece of healing for my current life. Now I am able to channel and mediate healing for others and help them unlock the puzzles in their lives which I find greatly rewarding.

It is impossible for me to convey all the beautiful co-creation of circumstances this gift has brought both for me and patients. I receive amazing correspondence full of healing stories telling me I am touching people's lives also remotely! I have yet to meet and work with some of the people who write me, yet they claim to have had dreams where I have appeared to them and see us working together! Those I do know also share with me how their own personal healing has touched others.

My personal experiences, clinical successes, and research in various Eastern healing arts has led me to the development of my method of healing, the Kousouli® Method, which I've taught to help thousands of patients achieve phenomenal results in my private practice. With the help of the higher power, I am grateful to share it with you and millions of people all over the world.

Chapter Two: History of Channeling Spirit

"The years teach much which the days never knew."
~ Ralph Waldo Emerson

Channeling Spirits and Guides has been around since the earliest cultures inhabited the earth. Archaeologists say all their major finds of primitive cultures have temples, or at least, special places to worship the Creator. Until modern religions (that branched off the Catholic Church) "banned" channeling as evil – and even looked at talking with Saints and Angels with disdain, channeling was practiced by many. The elders and wise men were often those who had practiced longest, so tribal people venerated them, and many acted as sages or gurus. Yet, going way back to Sumeria, Mesopotamia, Egypt and others in the pre-historic world, we see channeling was a normal practice.

The ancients on all continents have left tablets and pictographs that show they communicated in ways that included channeling. Spirits use whatever means they can to give people the messages they need to give, including dreams, visions, telepathy, letters, numbers, tea leaves, playing cards, Ouija Boards, radio signals, television screens, recorders, or charms and crystals; even a lucky rabbit's foot!

It doesn't matter what kind of tool the message comes by; the message is more important than the object used to deliver it. We don't care what kind of phone we use to get a loving call (or text message) from a family member we haven't heard from in a long time, as long as the message comes. It's the same with channeling. We can seek it, or it can come naturally. Some cultures used psychoactive chemicals from plants that have since been made illegal in many countries, including the United States.

American Indian tribes often used peyote in their vision quests. Used properly, Ayahuasca and Salvia divinorum have produced entrance into other realms.

But regulations have largely shut down the use of these plants for the obvious fact that those who use them gain insight and knowledge that threatens the status quo of those already in power, much like the Council did with the "words" of God, Jesus and the prophets.

Many have abilities both with the use of plant substances and remarkably, seemingly out of nowhere without them. Of course, 'nowhere' is really the Spirit world and contact can be initiated by spirits or by sensitive human beings. It can come either way.

The information obtained by channeling is neutral, neither good nor bad. It has both a good use and a bad use, depending on who is using the force of spirit. The rules of being good here in life also apply to using our free will to decide on what level you align with on the other side.

One example of a medium who used knowledge of his ability for good is Edgar Cayce, often referred to as "the sleeping prophet," (1877-1945) because he was able to answer questions about healing and disease, war, reincarnation, the sunken continent of Atlantis, and predict future event potentials while in a trance state.

The non-profit Association for Research and Enlightenment was founded in Virginia Beach to study and continue Cayce's work, where many use the knowledge of their "gifts" to the benefit of others.

Other more modern-day channels include Jane Roberts, Robert Butts, Ester Hicks, Lee Carol, Darryl Anka, and my mentor in channeling, Shawn Randall. Thanks to the Internet we can look them up and find out what they have accomplished to further our understanding of channeling.

The phenomenon of channeling appears to have been a part of everyday life in the pre-historic world of tribes that worshipped stars, gods and nature spirits we now think of as mythical. It only came under assault, first being called 'dangerous' and later even 'fraudulent,' around the time of the first Christian Councils.

Ancient Egypt is called the beginning of 'trance channeling' and 'dream channeling.' It is assumed by artifacts that prior to that time the natural world and the spirit world existed as one, with communication between them as the norm.

The ancient Chinese had trance channels called 'wu'. Philosopher Wang Ch'ung in the First Century spoke openly of dead spirits communicating through the living who were in a trance like state.

In ancient Greece, the spirits of death were called 'keres' and were thought to escape from jars in which corpses were stored. Around 540 B.C. Pythagoras also used a Ouija-board like instrument to communicate with spirits.

Mystery cults were often devoted specifically to the channeling of certain gods, and much Greek philosophy, especially that of Pythagoras and Plato, was full of it.

Oracles usually lived in caves because they thought at one time that the spirits came up from the underworld through crevices in rocks. References to "muses" were also channeled spirits as is evident in Homer's Odyssey.

Canon Law of the First Christian Churches Changed Thought Patterns

Only after the first Council of Nicaea in 325 A.D. was Christianity split into Roman and Greek factions and forms of 'Canon Law' begun. At this point, there had already been 33 Popes, and the first St. Peter's Basilica was in the process of being built. It was very much to the advantage of the Roman Emperor Constantine who organized the Council by inviting more than 1,000 Bishops and teachers of early Christianity because he knew this would solidify much of his territory through religious beliefs.

Early Canon Law stated which of the Jewish books would be accepted as part of Christianity, as it had begun to be called, and which early 'Christian' texts would be admitted into what became (eventually) the first Bible, and which would be thrown out.

So many things were accepted until that day simply because they had been passed down from far earlier cultures and were once a part of the people who followed Jesus. But once religion became organized, it was much to the advantage of early church leaders to block out anything that pointed toward spiritual practices and beliefs that would run counter to their laws. Obedience was taught - and forced - through fear and discrimination, later proven by so many bloody conquests made in the name of God. As recently as the 'conquering' of the United States by Europeans, hundreds of native cultures that respected old traditions and ways were obliterated from their land and forbidden to practice their religions.

But why, we ask? Why would so many things be simply thrown away? Why would people with 'special gifts' be 'banished' or burned at the stake, and in later times, ostracized and/or laughed at for showing they could connect with other realms; see the future; speak with Angels, Guides and Spirits, or heal using ancient means?

It all came down to power. But in the last 70 years, many began to think for themselves and leave belief systems that told them not to accept what they knew, felt and saw to be true.

In 1945 the Nag Hammadi Library was discovered in a small desert cave in Egypt. Since then, these have been called the Gnostic Gospels and 'banned' by organized Christian churches as evil. Yet the word 'gnostic' is simply 'knowledge' in Greek. These 'hidden' gospels mention all the old ways and cultures, bringing them back to life. They are believed to have been written between 200 and 400 A.D. and focus on the sayings of Jesus. In them, teachings claim a personal connection to the Father, without the need of organized religion. This would put the (formal) Church out of business.

Obviously, these books were hidden just after Bishop Irenaeus from what is now called Lyon, France, published his work, *Against Heresies,* in 180 A.D. It listed the books he considered heretical. Looking at them now, we can see they all talk of Jesus as someone who came as a wise-teacher who valued women as much as men and said human beings were created to do the same things "and more than these things shall ye do," that he did while here on Earth.

Working backwards, from Christianity to "the beginnings of channeling and other gifts," we see much mention of a marriage between astronomy and astrology; numerology and consulting with Angels, Spirits and Guides.

References to the numbers 3 and 12 were important in ancient texts and religious practices and in the Bible as well. Now known as numerology, it isn't hard to find examples proving how much these numbers were used in both the Old and New Testaments of today's Bible.

For instance, Noah had three sons; Job had three daughters; Daniel prayed regularly three times a day to God; later, Jesus said he would destroy the temple and rebuild it in three days (symbolically of course!); the well-known three wise men; three crosses on the hill; and the Trinity.

As for 12, which is mentioned 187 times in the Bible, we can easily see its importance by looking at the astrological chart as well as the months of the year. Twelve shows completion and the number itself, added together 1 plus 2 also equals 3.

Clearly, all religious holy texts are channeled information between man and God from earliest times. The Gospel of Thomas, one of the texts discovered in 1945 and "thrown out as heresy," gives one quote (Verse 39) from Jesus as, "The Pharisees and the scribes have taken the keys to knowledge and have hidden them. They do not go in, and they do not permit those desiring to go in to enter."

Many historians believe that many things were taken for granted back when Jesus spoke and that his sayings meant much more than modern day people realize. People think Jesus founded Christianity in its current form, but we must remember, Jesus was a Jew, and Christianity was founded by his followers after his death over a long period of time. Many words had different meanings, or interpretations then than they do now. Still, there are three instances mentioned in the Bible where communication with the dead is mentioned. (These probably slipped by the Councils).

Samuel 1-28: 6-20

Vs. 6: He (Saul) inquired of the Lord, but the Lord did not answer him by dreams or prophets. Saul then said to his attendants, "Find me a woman who is a medium, so that I may inquire of her."

The discussion of how this woman is found and what she says to Saul continues through Vs. 20.

Matthew 17: 1-8

Vs. 1: "After six days Jesus took with him Peter, James and John, brother of James, and led them up a high mountain by themselves. There he was transfigured before them. His face shone like the sun and his clothes became white as the light. Just then, there appeared before them Moses and Elijah, talking with Jesus."

The next seven verses talk of the conversation between those who came down from Heaven and those who were on the mountain.

Luke 16: 19-31

Vs. 19: "There was a rich man who was dressed in purple and fine linen and lived in luxury every day. At his gate was a beggar named Lazarus, covered with sores and longing to eat what fell from the rich man's table."

This story continues, and by verse 23, the rich man has died and (according to the text) is in Hell and called out to Lazarus who was with Abraham in a better place. He spoke to him and asked that he have pity on him. But Abraham speaks to him of his treatment of Lazarus while they were alive. Finishing the story, verse 31 states: "If they (people on Earth) do not listen to Moses and the prophets, they will not be convinced even if someone rises from the dead."

Thank goodness reason and a resurgence of the 'old ways' is returning.
The monotheistic thought patterns of religious worship for the last few centuries have gone from witch-burning to the cosmic searches of modern-day humankind. Many are beginning to realize that these 'special gifts' are built into the human mind and body and teachers have come through the ages to show us how to use them properly.

Where are we today? Although not yet in the full bliss of our spiritual power, a new age has definitely dawned. An age of re-discovery and sharing of information thanks to the internet and the mass awakening of humanity desiring a more purposeful existence with less hate and more love. Light workers are re-emerging fearless and passing the torch of knowledge to the next generation who will bring in more spiritual awareness of our Creator's love and truth. I hope my work here helps you grow to be part of this grand endeavor. Each of us must look deep inside and bring out our best - not just for ourselves, but also for our neighbor. We can forgo cursing the darkness since we can choose to shine our light instead.

Discovering who you truly are and how to tap into your inner power is a grand journey each must do by him/herself. If you're willing to try – go all the way. You must go all the way, otherwise it doesn't make sense to even start. Working with – and bringing forth - this inner power could mean losing people around you: spouses, lovers, or friends who don't understand your new-found growth. It could mean being disrespected, mocked, or isolated. Seeking one's inner light and personal connection to God is the greatest joy one can discover - there is no other feeling like it. Remember, it's not 'light-vacationer' it's 'light-worker'. Being a lightworker is tough at times. It pushes you, it stretches you, it makes you take a long hard look at yourself. It makes you challenge your darkest shadows and ask the hard questions. It digs in deep into the pain for new-found freedom. It's hard but rewarding work! Choose to begin…and let the synchronicities light your path.

Chapter Three: Aligned in Synchronicity

"Life is an unfoldment, and the further we travel the more truth we can comprehend. To understand the things that are at our door is the best preparation for understanding those that lie beyond."
~ Hypatia

Synchronicity is a term first introduced by psychologist Carl Jung, that talks about meaningful coincidences. When discussing spiritual topics, the word 'synchronicity' is used to describe things happening in a Divine (or Universal) order, with one thing leading to another until a pattern or purpose is revealed. It's a belief that things happen in certain ways to bring about something else that comes next, until a certain result has transpired.

We've all heard stories about someone having a car break down or some other event that makes a person miss his or her plane, or train, or ride to work. Then that plane, train or car suffers a catastrophe and everyone in it dies. But synchronicity can be subtler than that; like finding just the right information at just the right time or something or someone showing up just when you need what they have to say or give. It means looking at everything that happens and recognizing that there may be more than coincidence at work when things fall together one after another in a meaningful way.

Synchronicities show you are coming into alignment with a higher power. When people begin making connections with Spirit Guides or Angels or any being in another realm, it is especially important to be aware of small things that may be viewed as 'coincidence' because these beings come through in all kinds of ways. When you start to notice more of these in-sync moments, pause and take note. Perhaps a feather suddenly appears at your feet, you see 11:11 everywhere you turn, or you find something you've been looking for a long time right in plain sight where you know you could not have overlooked it previously.

We never know what the Spirits will do for us once we start trying to connect with them so it's always good to stay aware, so we don't miss something that later turns out to be just what we needed to get from "Point A to Point B."

Beyond the Five Senses

MIT researchers published a study April 19, 2016 in *Trends in Cognitive Sciences* that stated that human vision only echoes a small portion of what of what is actually seen.

"A ton of work supports that this perception that our visual experience is so rich and vivid is just totally wrong," said the study's first author, Michael A. Cohen, a postdoctoral fellow in the Nancy Kanwisher Lab at MIT's McGovern Institute for Brain Research.

Simply stated: There's a lot more to everything than we can see with our earthly eyes, although everyone has a built-in 'psychic' ability if developed.

We do not have five senses, we have more like 5000+, so Aristotle was wrong when he claimed in his book *De Anima* that "One might be confident that there is not another sense besides the five (vision, hearing, taste, touch and vision)." Unfortunately, my fellow Greek was not completely right, as he was only looking at the link between what was visible. However, if you take into account your sense of perception, which we know in chiropractic through proprioceptors in your joints, muscles and ligaments, play a huge role in notifying your body where it is in relationship to space. For proof, just put your hand out in front of your face with your eyes closed, and you know where it is, even if you can't see it. Also, you can walk with your eyes closed, without tripping, which is the same idea. We can agree then, that this is a sense, and it is a big omission of Aristotle's not to include that in his short list. Also, what about the feelings of heat and cold? We don't touch the fire or ice, but we can feel the energy coming from them. This is called thermoception. Pressure and pain can also be broken down to other subsenses. Balance and equilibrioception also involves the vestibular system with vision and proprioception together to help you maintain your balance. Different receptors send different signals to different parts of your brain. So, this begs the question…what else can you feel see or perceive? Is there a world beyond that you were taught to believe by your kindergarten teacher? When someone's dog is barking at the corner of the room, but you can't see anything there, is it because your pooch is picking up on sensations that you (as a human) haven't developed? When your parents told you to stop believing in that imaginary friend you knew you saw and with whom you were able to clearly communicate, were they not sensitive to what you were already able to pick up on? This begs us to ask the question, are we intrinsically built to have contact with the subtle energies around us, and do some people exercise their sensitivity, while others choose to be invulnerable to the esoteric sights and sounds of unseen friends around them?

Relevant Vocabulary and Concepts

Life Guides: The metaphysical use of Life Guides (or Spirit Guides) dates from early times and is still used by Spiritual believers and some religions and tribes all over the world. Many Native American Indian tribes venerate their Guides (also referred to as Grandfathers and Grandmothers or other ancestors). Some people use the term interchangeably with Angels, although the two are different in that Spirit Guides are said to have lived on the Earth in human bodies and volunteered to assist others after they moved on, while Angels are a different make of being and have not inhabited a human body. Life guides, angels and helpers from the non-physical realms are often referred to as our "**Unseen friends** or **Soul friends**." Life guides and human channels both know and choose who they work with by having a previous life connection, although the human channel doesn't cognitively know this until they start opening their spiritual capacities.

Meld or **Blending:** When the spirit of an unseen friend connects with the human channel for vocal channeling; a frequency step-down for the spirit world and a frequency step-up for the human to form a shared connection. A melding or blending is like when a device you want to connect for Wi-Fi searches for the device and once they find each other they communicate and lock in.

Angels: Often shown in art with wings, many people who have seen and talked with Angels say they often appear as human beings of light that can appear and disappear right in front of them in seconds. These beings are celestial, never having inhabited a human body (although they may appear human-like when seen by people on earth) and are said to come to the aid of humans in times of great need, sickness or fear.

Archangels: An Archangel is an Angel of high rank, often referred to as the 'head of an angelic army'. Catholics, Protestants, Jews, and other religions such as Zoroastrianism, Islam, Seventh-Day Adventists, and more all believe in these beings but differ on the number of Archangels that exist. Some believe there only to be one Archangel – Michael – while others have a whole list of names. Four of the most common Archangels are Michael, Gabriel, Raphael and Uriel.

Channel: The person who willfully connects through deep meditation to an unseen energy (guide or higher entity) and allows the entity a connection for communication from that world to this through their mind and body. Not a 'possession', as the channel is always in control of the event and may end communication with the unseen friend at any time.

Channeling: is when a (living) human being allows a spirit to come through his or her body and/or voice to give a message directly to another human being. This spirit can be a deceased loved one, a Spirit Guide, Ascended Master teacher, or someone from the angelic realm, to connect to a place of higher mind which brings forth information from 'out of this world'. Example: Being in 'the zone' playing a beautiful piece of music or performing a talent flawlessly, receiving genius insight or information that otherwise would not occur. Channeling is all about connection. It is about choice and free will to do so and 'knowing thyself'. And knowing thyself also leads to opening all answers to big questions like, "Where did I come from, what am I doing here, and most importantly, who am I to God?" A **channeling spirit** helps by giving needed information on any topic. Example: Insight on a life challenge or help in coping or finding closure to a friend or relative's physical death. The spirit will refer to its channel as their 'partner' when it refers to its physical human friend who channels. Relationship to the Divine is Channeling, a flowing smooth natural phenomenon. Resistance to channeling is a resistance to love which is the block in smooth soul communication.

Vocal Channeling: is relay channeling where you are the instrument of transmitting a message from an unseen friend with whom you have some type of past life or esoteric connection. The channel will use the vocabulary, experiences, knowledge and abilities (**the toolkit**) of the partner to relay the message. The scribes of the Bible or any holy text were all done by channeling messages from higher planes of knowledge.
Lower vibratory energies can, and do, work with people harboring lower emotional frequencies in their lives through the choices they make and their free will - they're simply 'invited in'.

Semiconscious or unconscious channeling with human filters gives an uncertain outcome. The goal to clear channeling is to drop all bias and human filters (anger, hate, jealousy, insecurity, unworthiness, fear, etc.) prior to connecting to attain a **pure loving message** from spirit. Any energy lesser than this, you are dealing with a lower less-desired entity. Alcohol intoxication and drug use also introduce lower vibrational energy. For more information on how to rebuke negative energies refer to my previous book *BE A MASTER® of Psychic Energy*.

The Holy Spirit never takes away your willpower or choice, never 'tells' you what to do, never scares or puts fear into you. It does however educate, love, protect, guide and give helpful information to strengthen you and empower your life's journey.

Resonance Causation is aligning yourself with the flow of Creation through trust. It can work positively or negatively based on the accumulation of energy already in one's awareness. Attraction of energies could summon good or bad. For example, multiple personality disorders are trauma-associated takeovers of the personality that can easily bring on more trauma, chaos and confusion. An afflicted person may give permission to lower vibratory energies to help them cope or 'protect' them during traumatic times to better deal with pain or loss. However, with time, this 'help' shows to be less than favorable to the inflicted channel and their situation worsens. In contrast, an accumulation of higher divine energy never carries a burden, but instead lifts the afflicted and keeps them away from harm.

Unseen Friend or **Soul Friend:** Subtle energies from the unseen realm that guide and protect you. These are usually those souls who have had a body at some time on earth which you knew or have never known in this lifetime but know them from a soul connection subconsciously during past lives lived. Doubters, skeptics, non-believers, or those not sensitive or unknowing of the spirit world tend to describe these as imaginary friends or figments of your imagination.

Medium: Someone who communicates between souls in the worldly realm and the spiritual realm. The medium, unlike the channel, who allows the spirit to speak directly, speaks by his or her own voice after hearing or seeing something given on the Other Side. The human individual conveys information seen, heard or felt rather than allowing the guide or spirit to speak for itself.

Mediumship: To communicate messages between the bodied and disembodied. Mediums work with spirits, guides, and deceased individuals to help complete unfinished business or to offer living people closure. Mediums are as much of service to the deceased as they are a help to those with bodies. Sometimes the energy coming from the deceased is too much for a medium to take directly, so channels ask the help of their unseen friends in channeled mediumship to vocally relay messages.

Channeled Mediumship: In channeled mediumship a channel communicates with guides who relay information vocally through the channel from the deceased. The guide does all the work, not the human medium. This helps buffer energy and allows for a healthy balance of energy between the disincarnate soul, the spirit guide, and the spirit guide's human channel. The unseen friend (spirit guide) plays 'middle man' to the communication and allows or disallows disincarnate energies to interact with the human channel.

Automatic Writing: A process where one meditates deeply and slides into a state where thoughts of an unseen friend automatically flow through to the hand of the channel and make it seem as if the hand is automatically writing by itself. The information coming through is of wiser and higher mind than the conscious person who normally writes in their waking state. The Holy texts were believed to have been auto-written by man through divine insight.

Higher Self: The divine power within that is also allied to the Universal Greater Consciousness that flows through all of creation. Also known as many names including the sacred self, the inner self, the higher consciousness, or the super-conscious mind; most belief systems believe there is an invisible, mysterious and wonderous aspect of ourselves that can deliver amazing miracles into our lives.

Affirmation Invocation: A statement you always proclaim to open the channeling session, set an intention and invite assistance with divine protection. An acknowledgement of oneness in resonance of environment; an invitation to allow your guide to talk to you and cut through the dimensions. The ancient way of doing this is conducting a lengthy and elaborate ritual or blood sacrifice. Churches are still very big on ritual; although no blood sacrifices, they do invite the holy spirit in by offering blessed bread and wine. Today ritual is done very quickly, seconds to minutes, through consciousness, intention and attention to the process with an open heart. For channeling, the affirmation invocation I personally use is:

"By the power of our Original Creator in Christ Consciousness, I now invite only my life guides, angels and archangels of highest good to speak clearly through me and to me with wisdom, truth, love and compassion. Any energies lesser than love are directed to the light. (In Greek - εἰς τὸ ὄνομα τοῦ Πατρὸς καὶ τοῦ Υἱοῦ καὶ τοῦ Ἁγίου Πνεύματος) In the name of the Father, Son and Holy Spirit, Amen."

Human Filter: A filter that skews the neutral or clear loving message from the unseen realm as it is delivered through the person channeling. Information coming through a channel should be as close to its original channeled source as possible, however a message from Divinity often picks up human bias on its way into our realm. Good channels maintain neutrality and don't edit the message while in transit or during delivery.

Spirit Board: Also known as a Ouija Board, which first appeared in stores in the 1890's, is a flat piece of plastic, wood or metal material that has letters of the alphabet and numbers zero through nine imprinted on it which the unseen friend focuses on with a planchette or arrow indicator. In a quiet setting, sometimes called a seance, a person asks a question while resting his or her hands on the planchette. Then the planchette is moved to letters that spell out the message the spirit answering wishes to give to someone in the room. The spirit board is just a tool, and as with any tool, a tool can be used with good, or bad, intent. Religious organizations tend to shun its use by focusing on the negative aspects with fear to keep uneducated people away from connecting to higher knowledge. Hollywood also sensationalizes and sells many horror movies based on its mystery.

EVP, Electronic Voice Phenomenon: A well-known phenomenon in parapsychology and 'ghost hunting' where spirit records its voice onto electronic recordings as communications to those in this realm that seek connection through questions posed to spirits. The spirit has to download its energy into our dense reality here. While we must at the same time upgrade our sensitivity to hearing and feeling Spirit in order to communicate clearly. This divide is usually called "the veil". Since spirits are an energy, one of the easiest ways they can interact with us is through electrical signals. They can affect lightbulbs, radio and television static, or imprint their energy signal onto magnetic tape recorders which can be heard as a human voice.

Your Guides Are Always There, Helping You Create Your Journey

I relied on the laws of the Universe and helpful divine intervention to manifest my career, everything from good grades on tests to the diploma; to find mentors and create my Beverly Hills office space, and many living spaces in Los Angles that I wanted. My guides have helped me tremendously with my health, manifesting the doctors and timing for rapid healing through two major heart surgeries. So many worries were going through my mind, but those worries led to simplicity after trusting and praying that my guides take my hand and lead the way. There are countless times they have proven to me that there is something outside my limited human 3-D linear perception that is guiding me, and these synchronistic events and good fortune are not mere coincidence.

Your loving guides do not take over your free will. They will only intervene if you sincerely ask them to while getting your ego out of the way. They do not live your life or do your work for you, but they can help make connections along your path, so your life feels much smoother. They are able to bring a lot of the 'wow' factor we as humans want to experience but may fall short of experiencing due to our frustrations and shortcomings.

Here are some amazing circumstances I can't believe were just chance or luck, and I credit my guides for their involvement in making me a believer through the decades.

Orbs in Photos May Be Guides Making a Cameo

Have you ever taken a photo and seen a blob that looks like circular smudge? There have been a lot of studies about this orb phenomenon and they have

concluded it is not dust in the lens, light refracting at a certain angle or a figment of one's imagination. It's very real. "The Orb Project" by Klaus Heinemann Ph.D. and Míceál Ledwith Ph.D. presents data collected after they researched thousands of photos to test the hypothesis that the light circles were actually spirit beings. Once you start on a path of inner discovery, don't be surprised if your life guides, angels and/or archangel decide to take a selfie with you… just to let you know they're there. Another big way spirit guides show you they are with you, is aligning you in miraculous synchronicities.

Guides Help Beautify My First Office Space

Years ago, when I left my associateship with my third mentor of chiropractic in Beverly Hills to start my solo practice, I had an amazing story of synchronicity occur, that to this day brings a huge smile to my face. I had leased out a small space in Beverly Hills to start my first wellness center. The space was very small and the rent was very high, as would be expected in Beverly Hills. To make my small wellness center work, I knew I had to make it special. It had to have a very welcoming energy and look beautiful. So, I set out to make it so. One day I took my girlfriend to a popular spa that everyone liked and there I looked for clues why people enjoyed going there. One thing jumped right out at me; the wallpaper. It was gorgeous. It had a shimmer in it and crystals that sparkled as you moved; it looked like angel wings were moving as you moved with it. In lower light conditions it was even more breathtaking. I had to have that in my newly (being built) office, my patients would love it! I asked the spa owner where they sourced it from, and it had been so long ago he couldn't give me the information. But to be honest, he probably didn't want me to know as it was so unique! So, I looked everywhere to find this wallpaper in Los Angeles. No one seemed to have it. I had exhausted all the stores and was about to give up. However, I had one store I hadn't gone to yet.

I called my designer and we went to the shop together. I tried to explain to the shop employee the exact characteristics of the wallpaper I was desperately seeking. He didn't know and went to get the manager. When the manager came out he was wearing a shirt with a big cross prominent in the style of the shirt, and it stuck out loudly getting my attention. I explained to him again what I told the employee. His face lit up and said, "oh yes, we were the ones who did that spa's décor". He continued: You have expensive taste - that's one of the most expensive wallpapers around. It's about three thousand per roll because we have to ship it from Germany, so it'll be about eight weeks to get here." My heart sank. I was not able to afford three thousand for wallpaper or wait for anything to ship from Germany in eight weeks because my office had to be ready in one week! I was seeing few patients and finances were not in good shape at all. "We may have some of that I think in stock, let me check." My designer was skeptical, and I was starting to doubt as well. We started to look at our wall lengths and measurements while the manager went to the back room to check. I had to do my waiting room in beige and the treatment room in white. Since the space was small we didn't need much so I hoped that we could find another wallpaper there that would work if the one I wanted wasn't available. We waited about ten minutes and then the manager comes to us and said: "One of those Ocean's Eleven or Thirteen movie set designers used this same wallpaper, so yes, I have some left in stock back there. However, the bad news is we only have this length in beige and this amount in white, sorry guys." My designer and I were at a loss for words. The manager without his knowing, just put in front of us the exact amounts we needed plus a little extra, to complete the wallpaper installation with the exact wallpaper I wanted. Still in shock and with my heart beating a mile a minute, I said, "we'll take it, but how much?" He said, "Well, since I don't have to get it shipped and it's already here, I'll give you a discount on it all. How about $1,100 for everything including tax?" I said, "Sold!"

Now still in awe about what had just happened, we went to the office to leave the wallpaper for the installers to put up during the weekend. While there I had my designer help me assemble a beautiful wooden bench for the waiting room. My designer was built like a lumberjack, strong and big boned, as he also had a construction background. He was easily double the size of me, and I'm a pretty decent size guy at 5'11, 195 pounds. I heard him huffing and puffing about getting some screws into a tough part of the wood's joint assembly. As I looked in to see in the room he was working in, I asked, "what's going on?" he exclaimed, "It's not going in! My knuckles are scraping, and this damn screw isn't going anywhere. The screw head is getting stripped!" I walked over calmly to the half-inserted screw, asked him to hand me the screwdriver, and with an appreciation and gratefulness for what I had witnessed earlier that day with the wallpaper gift from Spirit, I prayed and thought to myself, "God, you can do anything, and this is nothing." With that in my heart and mind, with a calm confidence I proceeded to turn the screw into the wood as if hot metal was going through butter. My designer gasped at the sight of me - without any resistance - being able to get that screw head flush with the wood's surface. With his eyes bulging, he got up and walked out yelling, "I don't know how you do it man, I don't know how you do it." I thought to myself, I didn't do it, something far greater did.

Angel Manifests Rose Petal During Treatment

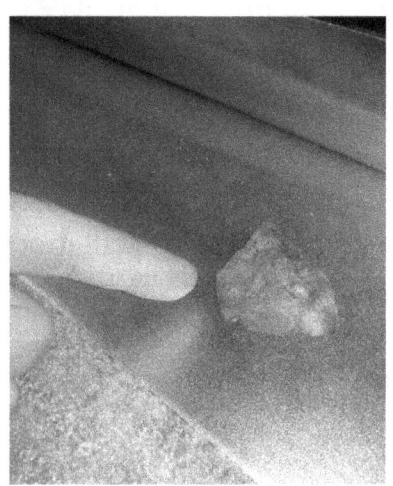

As I was about to conclude a therapy session with a long-time patient, a miraculous thing occurred which still to this day keeps me in amazement. The patient had been a long-standing student and had grown considerably in her spiritual evolution, yet she expressed that she had a hard time getting a certain negative person out of her mind and wanted a tangible exercise to deal with this when situations came up during her day at work. I told her about the flower petal tool, which I go into detail about in my book, *BE A MASTER® of Psychic Energy*. I continued, "To use this psychic meditation tool, envision a large flower petal, a pink rose petal for instance – and you see yourself surrounded by it as the negative energy is coming at you. Now since the rose petal is a neutral loving symbol it does not act like a bubble or fire wall which most people use to 'protect themselves' from negative psychic attacks. Pink rose balances out the negative energy with love without producing other negativity in the process. Different colors like green or yellow denote different energy vibrations. Use a pink rose petal for your circumstance, and that should do the trick. Now, as you do use the pink rose petal and it gets blasted with negative energy, you will see the petal turn brown and weak. When this happens, it's time to freshen up your connection by putting up new, pretty, healthy rose petals for further protection. Let the brown used ones just fall away." Just as she thanked me and was about to get up we looked down and couldn't believe what we were seeing. A pink rose petal that was worn away and brown in some areas. I snapped a photo with my cell phone to capture the exact moment, before she picked it up as this was just unbelievable to us both. The photo is the exact rose petal. There were no flowers in the office at that time, and I'm convinced this was placed there by one of our guides. There is no other explanation, a PINK ROSE PETAL (not red, white or any other color) just appeared exactly as I had discussed with her; and BROWN in spots and looking "used up" just as I had moments ago described! Incredible!

Billboard-Sized Notions

Driving through Palm Springs, California, I one day glanced over at a billboard while stopped in traffic. It was a very unimpressive sign with some lame advertisement by a not so fascinating cowboy on it. I remember saying, "wow, anyone can be on a billboard these days," and thought I could give a better presentation and message by being on the billboard. I thought, "Oh come on, I should be on a billboard. Ha! At least I'd have something worthwhile to present," and that was that, the light turned green and I was on about the rest of my day. I totally forgot about it until about eight months later I got a call from a friend of mine who wanted me to do some modeling as a caregiver for a nursing home, in a magazine ad. I agreed to it and did the shoot, thinking nothing of it. I later was told that the owner of the ad wanted to make that photo a billboard and asked if I minded being blown up and put on a billboard. Well, the rest is history.

Requesting a Specific Romance

Desiring to date a specific type of woman for my next romantic relationship, I meditated as I created the union in my mind and formed a vision board. I chose a photo of myself that was looking forward at the camera. I then cut out a woman kissing someone in a magazine cologne ad. Instead of them kissing, I connected the two photos of us so that she was kissing me on the cheek as I smiled. I posted us onto my vision board. About six months later I started dating exactly the description of what I had put down I sought in a mate physically and personality-wise. The facial features, dark beautiful hair, big eyes, beautiful lips, curvy body and long legs were all accounted for. Every time she took a photo of us she unknowingly posed in that SAME pose of kissing me on the cheek and taking the photo. It wasn't once, or twice. It was almost every time she took a photo with me. It became evident to me once I compared my vision board to the photos of us together that I had manifested her into my reality. Of the twenty things I had requested as characteristics for a mate on the board, the guides provided a lady with sixteen of them. It would be later shown to me that those four missing things and a few others I forgot to ask for in my presentation on the board, were the reasons we fell out of that relationship. Our thoughts really do manifest our reality; our guides are a big part of helping the process happen quickly. This exercise and more like it, can be found in the book *BE A MASTER® of Your Reality*.

Spirit Saves the Clinic

It was the second year of practicing on my own and I had overspent my budget on various things I didn't need along with it being a very slow winter quarter, and I dreaded every day as the close of the month of December crept up. Living paycheck to paycheck the stress of being an entrepreneur holistic healer in Beverly Hills doing it all myself, caught up to me. I was seriously in the red and rent was due in a few days. I didn't have any patients scheduled for treatment and so there was no paycheck anywhere in the foreseeable future. I was so stressed. I remember saying to myself, "that's it. I'm going to have to close my doors and the business has failed. I have failed. I gave it a try. But, I don't want it all to end like that. I have to keep the doors open, my people need me! I just don't know what I can do, tomorrow rent is due, and I owe over $2,000." I had two days grace period to get the rent check in, so I started to write a letter to the landlord about my financial situation and the whole time my insides were in pain. I cried out, "Help, I need help, God help, I don't want to do this!" Literally that moment, I received a call from a patient I hadn't seen in a few months. Are you in the office today?" She asked. "Yes, I am, how can I help you?" She said, "I'm driving by your office in a few minutes and have this check still here from my personal injury case that settled few months ago, my lawyer gave it to me and I haven't been able to drop it off to you. Thank you for taking such good care of me after my accident, I feel great! I can drop it off if you're there." "I'm here, oh I'm here! I'll be expecting you. How much is the check for may I ask?" "It's for $4,000," she said. I tore up the letter to the landlord, laughing deliriously and so grateful for the miracle I just received. Ask and you shall receive.

Guides Leave Their Calling Card

I was lucky enough to have the convenience of living near my office several years back, so I took advantage of walking fifteen minutes to the office instead of driving. One beautiful sunny day, I was really enjoying the weather as I passed by a vine with flowers and roses, I paused and took a quick sniff. I remember how grateful I felt for the life I lived. I thought to myself, "You really are doing what you love and are happy. We're going to the office to help people. The feeling inside me was one of warmth and connection. I then said out loud, "Hey angels, I know you're with me right now, but I really would like a sign of some sort." I laughed as I just kept walking. I reached my office building, and right before I got to the elevator, I looked down and saw the sign I had asked for. A beautiful white feather. This feather to this day sticks out of my business card holder, as a reminder on my desk, they are always with me. Patients ask me all the time about the feather when they see it on my desk. One day a new patient who didn't know about the feather story came up to the office. She was smiling and excited to start her care plan. I saw her holding a little feather. I asked her, "Where did you get that feather?" "I just found it at the base of the elevator," she said.

Guides Provide Proof and a Meal

Specifically asking for synchronicity from my guides as an act of abundance, I requested a gesture to show me they were with me. Also, I was getting a little hungry and asked if the gesture could be a meal. As I was thinking this, I was also walking by a convenience store. I went in to check some lottery tickets I had forgotten were in my back pocket. After noticing the bonus numbers both being eleven - I won on both tickets! I laughed out loud about the 11-11 synchronicity and the merchant looked at me funny, but I didn't care. I added my winnings to the lonely two dollars I already had crumbled in my pocket. I left and went to the restaurant next door and got the meal I asked for. Again, I asked, and I received. Speak to your guides as if you would talk to a best friend who is with you. They are indeed there. If you ask with an open heart while keeping a child-like playfulness, don't be surprised when they respond.

This One's on Us; Movie Paid for by My Guides

I got a call from a friend to go see a 3D movie after work, it was starting at 11 P.M. and I told him to get me a ticket as I would run straight to the theatre to meet him after work and wouldn't have time to get a ticket. I asked him if he could spot me the twenty dollars for the movie, I'd pay him right back. I left the office in a rush to meet him. As I reached into my pocket

to grab some cash, I thought I had the twenty. I apologized when I realized I only had a five and some singles. I told him, no worries, I knew I had some money in my car console also, so I would get him the total as I gave him a ride home later. After the movie I looked into the console and to my disappointment and shame I couldn't keep my promise of paying my friend back and said to him apologetically, "I am going to have to pay you tomorrow, so sorry, I thought I had enough, but I only have thirteen total and some change here. I thought I had larger bills." He said, "no worries, of course pay me back whenever you can." We were in a very good mood after the movie, as we had both enjoyed it very much. My friend is also a believer and light-hearted guy with a child-like energy, so our conversations always revolve around manifestation and talking of the higher power's action in our lives. As we ended our day's fun and I was about to stop the car to drop him off, I saw in the not-so-distant-front of my car a white paper, or what looked like trash shining off my headlight's beam. A whisper in my ear, said otherwise, "That's your twenty." With astonishment I told my friend, "see that piece of paper there by the curb – check to see if that's a twenty. I have a feeling it is." My friend was laughing so hard as he was getting out of the car, thinking no way that was true, but he humored me by walking towards it. His face went from disbelief to pure, 'you got to be kidding me!' As he picked up the twenty-dollar bill. "I don't know how you did that, but I guess the Universe just paid for your movie ticket." He immediately grabbed his cell phone as I raised my movie ticket for a shot to mark the moment, as we were both in shock and awe of what just happened.

Earlier in the day I had connected with my guides through channeling and spoke to them about alignment. They explained to me the more you are in alignment, the more it will show as coincidences that are in fact not coincidences at all, but an alignment with Source energy. I had specifically asked about seeing the occurrence of numbers like 11:11 a lot more often. The movie was at 11 P.M., I even sat in seat number twenty for the movie, and my guide supplied a twenty-dollar bill to cover my movie cost. Alignment was shown to us both, and both our minds were blown.

Guides Show Their Presence Through Music

A few months after a breakup in 2016, I was cleaning my bedroom on a Saturday morning, and as I dusted off a shelf, found a postcard marked with a love note and photo of an ex-girlfriend and me kissing. I felt love for her sharing that moment with me and thought to send her blessings; wishing her well. Although not meant for each other, we shared fun times and helped each other learn a lot about ourselves. I smiled, felt gratitude for that relationship and how we both grew. At that very moment the song on the radio station I had on sounded the lyrics "this time last year" and looped over and over with a very happy tune. Glancing at the clock, the time was 11:11 am; I burst into laughter. It was exactly that time last year that we had met. I kept smiling knowing I was not alone in that room and my guides were there to help me reconnect to the feeling of gratitude and love. And they continue to remind me when I glance at the clock or a license plate finds my periphery, of the 11:11 or 111 alignment.

Hollywood Dreaming

A while back, before I became a full-time dedicated healer, I was considering staying in my prior profession, photography and videography. I had a small, just budding, boutique production company that would cater to entertainers and help them prepare their image portfolios for the talent agencies for a career in modeling and acting. I was debating creating a new ad for marketing and promotion that involved models, a mansion, a large video and photography crew, luxury cars and a pool. My budget was close to a few hundred dollars at best. I envisioned grand doors opening up in a scene where beautiful models would escort the photographer through the doors to the backyard party for a photoshoot. I envisioned it and thought this would be a very alluring video to intrigue people into seeking out my work and separate me from the crowd of competition. I let go of the vision after I had spent a lot of time daydreaming about it but could not act on the daydream due to a lack of funds. Two years later I found myself in California where I met an editor from a large production company and I pitched to him that idea on a whim asking him what he thought about it. He said, "shouldn't be hard to do and I'd like to do it - for next to free!" I couldn't believe this major video editor wanted to do it for almost no cost when he gets paid thousands for his work. He explained to me that he wanted fun projects to get his mind off all the other boring assignments his clients gave him. He was as excited as I was to work on it. That rolled the ball and before I knew it everything divinely came into place and each step just fell into the next one. The model calls were made out, and the models wanted to be part of the production for free just to have it for their reels, the estate was one of the model's boyfriend's places and it, and their luxury convertible were given to us to use for free. Makeup artists gave of their talents freely, and The Universe provided everything for zero or very little cost; everyone wanted to be a part of the grand vision. Everyone had so much fun, and I got my grand door entrance with models escorting me into the pool party, just as my linear human 'ego' mind had envisioned. It was two years after I had the thought that it all manifested, but I realized what happened at that moment and how manifestation is something we do control while our guides help bring it all together for us. The rate of how quickly it manifests depends on several factors, including a feel-good fun factor, an 'everyone wins' mentality, and other steps mentioned in depth in *BE A MASTER® of Psychic Energy*.

Angels Connecting Healers to Those Seeking Healing

I needed to have an Internet connection hooked up at my place and was waiting for the technician to arrive for my appointment time. The technician comes and tells me his name is Rafael. Rafael is an archangel's name as well, who oversees prayers for healing, AND I had just left my bank, where I met a teller named Gabriel who has the same name as the archangel with the duty of sending messages and delivering strength. So, as I am going about my work at my place, the technician overhears a call come in for me. It is my editor and we are discussing a book as it is being written for changes and upgrades. After I finish my call, he asked me if I am a writer. I said yes and told him what I do. He opened communication and told me that he was seeking a healer but was very confused and lost about who to go see. I asked if I could work with him and ask his guides for information. He agreed, and as I asked and worked over him, a heat came through us and we started to sweat. He was overcome with gratitude after I told him about the specific traumatic event, right down to the age his problem started, that he had been stricken with a fear vibration that had caused his current health issue. Everything made perfect sense to him, and after giving him action steps to take to correct it, he went his way. Scenarios like these happen weekly where people are led to me for guidance, and if all hold open hearts and minds, Angelic forces can come through with big synchronistic results.

Chapter Four: Learning from the Master

"The most exquisite paradox… as soon as you give it all up, you can have it all. As long as you want power, you can't have it. The minute you don't want power, you'll have more than you ever dreamed possible."
~ Ram Dass

To reach a level of mastery it takes at least ten years to perfect most crafts, and other detailed specialties like surgery, a lifetime. Likewise, channeling Spirit may be something really easy for some while highly challenging for others who may just not have the complete tool box built into their DNA. Some can pick up a new trade or skill quickly, while others can't screw in a lightbulb or change a tire if their lives depend on it. It takes many elements to become sensitive and confident enough to be a healthy channel. There is one important trait that all great people who pass human limits show us; that is what can happen when we possess a concrete belief in the higher power.

Changing your limited and outdated belief system is paramount in allowing yourself the ability to channel. Everyone who has the extrasensory perception of connecting to spirit is open to the idea of other worldly communication. Every culture, country and time era has had its own leader of spiritual power to look up to. As a Christian, I look at how Jesus Christ of Nazareth himself connected to his higher power, the undeniable power of the Father.

Here are some powerful Bible verses demonstrating Jesus's connection to communicating with the Father and doing wonderous acts of healing through his immense belief.

John 16:28

"I came forth from the Father and have come into the world; I am leaving the world again and going to the Father." *Jesus explains that his energy and spirit is not of this earth and he will continue to exist after his physical death by returning to the source origin.*

John 6:38
"For I have come down from heaven, not to do My own will, but the will of Him who sent Me." *Jesus explains his human form did not bring him here, rather it was his higher energy state that chose the human form to create in this realm the mission he had set forth.*

John 5:19
"Therefore Jesus answered and was saying to them, "Truly, truly, I say unto you, the Son can do nothing of Himself, unless it is something He sees the Father doing; for whatever the Father does, these things the Son also does in like manner." *Meaning that we are "from 'and of" the power that made us, made in the likeness of our Father, and that we, and the Son and the Holy Spirit are bound as one.*

John 10:30
"I and the Father are one." *Has the same meaning as above, John 5:19.*

John 6:44
"No one can come to Me unless the Father who sent Me draws him; and I will raise him up on the last day." *Your inner power comes from your Creator, and at the end of your physical life this energy goes back to its source origin.*

John 14:28
"You heard that I said to you, 'I go away, and I will come to you, ' If you loved Me, you would have rejoiced because I go to the Father, for the Father is greater than I." *The unseen energy that we all are from - the Father source, is far greater in power than the physical form we see here on Earth.*

Matthew 26:39
"And He went a little beyond them, and fell on His face and prayed, saying, "My Father, if it is possible, let this cup pass from Me; yet not as I will, but as You will." *Here we see Jesus communicating with an unseen higher-level energy beyond this realm; which all Christian churches accept.*

Matthew 4:19

"Come, follow me," Jesus said, "and I will send you out to fish for people." *Those who choose to have a direct relationship with the higher power will be blessed to teach and help others also see the power within.*

Mark 11:24-25

"Therefore I tell you, whatever you ask for in prayer, believe that you have received it, and it will be yours. And when you stand praying, if you hold anything against anyone, forgive them, so that your Father in heaven may forgive you your sins." *This is the 'Law of Attraction' as explained in his day. Holding no grudges lightens our hearts so we can fully manifest our power.*

Matthew 5:10

"Blessed are those who are persecuted because of righteousness, for theirs is the kingdom of heaven." *Those who have opened their hearts and minds to the truth will know of realities others do not understand. Believers will be persecuted and ridiculed for their position, but they will find comfort in God's righteousness.*

John 14:6

"Jesus answered, "I am the way and the truth and the life. No one comes to the Father except through me." *You cannot understand vast spiritual truths and your connection to the other side – the unseen, unless you first live a loving life and understand these teachings you are being shown. Be as Jesus was. Follow his example.*

If you pick up a newspaper from 50 years ago the information now is worthless, with nothing of value to your life. But pick up the words of Christ and the wisdom is as applicable now as it was then. He tells us that He is "the way, the truth and the life" in John 14:6 and understanding the meaning of this for the application in our own lives has remarkable power. He shows us by His example.

Matthew 19:14
"Jesus said, "Let the little children come unto me, and do not hinder them, for the kingdom of heaven belongs to such as these." *Interestingly enough, we are told that being child-like in spirit, with a 'childlike' innocence (being an unburdened soul), is inappropriate in our society - yet, this is the key for joy and love!*

Matthew 19:26
Jesus looked at them and said, "With man this is impossible, but with God all things are possible." *What the limited linear ego mind of man can't do, the multidimensional mind of the higher power can.*

The wealth of knowledge in the Gospels demonstrates Jesus connecting to an otherworldly power that was able to command physics unlike anyone else. From the healing of the leper in Galilee (Matthew 8:1-4, Mark 1:40-45, Luke 5:12-15), to removing negative spirits from afflicted people's energy fields such as in Matthew 8:28-34, Mark 5:1-15, Luke 8:26-39, or performing feats that defied logic such as multiplying several fish and bread to feed five thousand hungry mouths as mentioned in Matthew 14:13-21. The Christ used senses and abilities far past the five we learned of since Aristotle's time. Over the centuries many have been able to tap into the power of the super senses, as Jesus himself told his disciples (and followers) they could.

John 14:12-14
"Very truly I tell you, whoever believes in me will do the works I have been doing, and they will do even greater things than these, because I am going to the Father. And I will do whatever you ask in my name, so that the Father may be glorified in the Son. You may ask me for anything in my name, and I will do it."

Jesus also tells us that through his teachings we can remove all the negatives in our lives as the information shared is the power itself to remove all evil.

Luke 10:19

"Behold, I give unto you power to tread on serpents and scorpions, and over all the power of the enemy: and nothing shall by any means hurt you."

If any master showed people the way to a better life through a connection with the higher power, it indeed was the Christ. Why do so many then, miss understanding the powerful information available to them by not tapping into the power of communication with their guides, angels and archangels? God and his messengers are here to help us every day. All we need to do is open our minds and ask them to speak and then listen to hear what they say.

Chapter Five: Making Contact

*"You be good. That's your business. The rest, leave to God.
That's his business."*
~ Fakeer Ishavardas

It is only possible to communicate with angels and spirit guides - in fact anyone on the Other Side - if we stay open and willing to let our analytical mind go. If we hold negative emotions or feel really "different or weird" about what we are trying to do, it just won't happen. We must realize that everyone has these abilities from childhood. It is the world, society's environment, that shuts down these natural abilities. All we are doing is opening ourselves back up to capabilities we should have had active all along. Because of what society has said about the capability to connect with spirit, many hide their ability.

Just realize you aren't going crazy, but instead reopening to your childhood wonder and connectivity, which has always been there - just covered with doubt and the hard 'realities' of this dense dimension called human life. If you have been hiding your gift of spirit connection, in order to allow yourself the experience of the challenges, the ups and downs, let go now and allow yourself to rise like a phoenix! Don't allow those who have buried their abilities keep you from unearthing yours!

Ask your spirit guides to show you the synchronicities. Synchronicities like Déjà vu are there to get your attention throughout life and to remind you that you are in an illusion that you have created. You must love and value the 'human' self to connect with higher self and unseen friends. These are tools and skills of consciousness. You must allow wonder and awe, without getting in the way.

Try saying something like: "I step myself aside. I allow you to speak clearly and loudly so I can understand." Or: "How can I be more open, feel more deserving and willing so that you can come to me?"

Many people keep their ability to channel and use their extrasensory abilities to themselves due to fear, thoughts of worthlessness, feelings of not being deserving, and low self-esteem. Choose to let go of what others think and open your abilities by dedicating time to the process.

Without constant practice and help from a knowledgeable and experienced instructor, the process of channeling can be quite intimidating to the beginner. In many cases a deep spiritual and mental fog must be cleared first before receiving a little bit of confirmation from your guides that you're on the right path. Frustrations and daily earthly distractions can easily derail any progress made if not diligent and deeply yearning for a personal connection to God. Though if persistent, the door will be opened to you - as is promised in the Bible:

Matthew 7:7–8
"Ask, and it shall be given to you; seek, and ye shall find; knock, and it shall be opened unto you: For every one that asketh, receiveth; and he that seeketh findeth; and to him that knocketh, it shall be opened."

General Guidelines That Help in Clear Spirit Communication

Through personal communication with my spirit guides and experience in clairvoyance, I found these tips helpful when applied to channeling. Keeping these in mind can help you focus on the high vibrational frequency needed to communicate and build a stronger channeling connection.

- Good spirits are very loving. They will always give you honest and true responses even if your ego gets bruised a little. They give it to you straight. With me, Tony the light 'energy' guide has a very direct 'this is how it is' way of presenting information. Heroditus, my past life healer guide, presents his information in a way that is more rounded out, making you think deeply about his reply. Every energy has their own unique characteristic communication and delivery system. Positive energies will ALWAYS let you live your own life and won't dare to cross the line in taking away your free will.

- Happy spirits love to have fun and can have a great sense of humor! They can indeed joke with you or lovingly poke at you from the Other Side. Both Tony and Heroditus do so with me in communications you will read of in chapter eight. However, this is always done with love and in respectful ways - never in a mean, demeaning or hurtful way.

- Take good care of yourself and rest. In the beginning, when I tried to channel I was too tired to after work. It did affect the speed of communication. So, you must be well rested, nourished, hydrated and focused when working with spirit. Intent and a lot of energy are used to communicate messages from beyond. Correct diet and steps to open up clairvoyance have been included in *BE A MASTER® of Psychic Energy*.

- Don't be rude or demanding with your spirit guide. Always respect the spirit like you would an elder or good friend who is helping you. They actually are here to help you in your reality as they learn lessons in their own plane of existence at the same time. Just as if you would show respect to a fellow human being, they want to be respected. You will find them willing to help you when you are lovingly respectful to them. If you are rude or ask unimportant questions, the communication is less strong. It's as if you ask your friend a bad question and they give you a puzzled look like "really?"

- Always begin and end your sessions with a prayer so you and the communication stay in a high positive vibration. Never channel when you are depressed, on drugs, drunk, angry, grieving, needy or in any state less than 100 percent loving and happy. Channel only when your energy is at its highest joy, as then you will attract the right guides. If you are in a low vibration, you will attract less than optimal guidance.

You wouldn't ever want to stand outside your door and invite an evil stranger into your home (in this case your body and mind). It's the same concept here, open the invitation only to good energies worthy of you and your space.

- Sometimes your usual personal life guides will step aside to allow another teacher to come in and help you for a short period of time, depending where you are on your life's journey. They will return in time. In chapter eight you will read about my healer guide's explanation on this transition, when he allowed another guide to add to the teachings.

- BE PATIENT. Your spirit guides are learning to lower their frequency vibration to our density just as we have to learn to speed up our vibratory frequency towards theirs. We meet halfway and our focused intent allows the communication to occur.

- Loving spirits and guides who you want to connect with will NEVER trick you into worshiping them or dedicating a ritual to them. They will ALWAYS speak highly of Jesus Christ, the Saints, the works of the Bible, the Trinity, Gospels and Father God. They will always praise God and point you toward the love and light of Christ Consciousness. Bad spirits want to appeal to your ego and may become very pushy over time. They give you bad advice and wish you to harm yourself or others. If you ever encounter anything blaspheming or speaking negatively of the powers of light and love, you are dealing with an evil or lower level spirit which is not in alignment with your highest good. Immediately pray, send them to the light of God for cleansing, say goodbye, end the session and disconnect all further communication with them. Return to your guides and spirit communication after deep meditation and prayer at another time when you are much clearer, lighter and joyful.

- Although guides are on the other side and are privy to much more awareness than we are, it is important to know that <u>they are NOT always correct and mistakes from both sides can be made</u>. While they do their best to guide, they are also learning to help and participate in their own growth as well. Also, depending on the tool you use to communicate with your guides, as well as the length of time you have communicated - both - will influence how well the data flows into your understanding. They have to take multidimensional probabilities, package, deliver and describe data as best they can to our linear-thinking dense human reality. At the start, it's going to always be awkward, murky and less frequent communication. Give it time, as you are both working on establishing your matching frequency. The soul does not end after physical death here on Earth, it does move on to further expand its creation. Guides also vary on many levels of experience with both their gifts and their wisdom. We do vary which guides throughout our life help us - depending on what challenges we face. Some people will be working with 'rookie' guides while others who need more guidance in larger works will connect with master teachers and healers.

Our unseen friends are always watching over, helping and protecting us. A greater, higher version of each of us is there when we sleep, eat, have fun, cry, do good or bad; are with our lover, picking our nose and yes, even when we're on the toilet or taking a shower. They're always there. Always non-judgmental, always loving. Through the good, the bad and the ugly, they are willing to move energy for you, help your desires manifest, assist in any way that is in your highest good. However, you must take action steps that are within your control and of your creation, to give them permission to act on your behalf, as they do not work against your God-given free will. This means that if you want some experience in your life - good or bad (by our human perception) they won't get in the way of you desiring to bring forth that experience. If an experience increases your soul's expansion, they see it as fit and good – no matter what hardship the human mind may think is a travesty. Spirit lovingly supports your growth, even if on a human level it seems 'bad' or 'awful' - on a spiritual level it's all about learning and growing. This explains a lot of the "Why isn't God listening" comments many say when they are frustrated. Or, "Why would God let bad things happen to a good person?" - like disease, loss of a loved one, bankruptcy, or other seemingly negative happenings. Well, God has given everyone free will to choose his or her path and make their own decisions. Guides and angels help but it's the person's own choices and soul searching that guide the mix of possibilities. Now multiply that by over seven plus billion people in our world and the co-creative process of everyone sending and receiving desires, and that will explain the condition of the world we are in. Imagine what could be done if everyone banded together and asked for world peace. It would get done with swift response.

Top Eight Questions You Should Ask First, Once You Connect

In my experience contacting my guides, I found it very helpful to have a list of questions at the ready to start a dialogue. Many in the beginning don't have any idea what to say or ask. Begin dialogue and tailor it once a relationship is formed. These questions should help start you off.

1. Hello. What is your name, or how may I refer to you?

2. Are you from the highest vibration of love and light? *If the spirit says yes, go to the next question. If it says no, you have connected to a lower entity and you should dismiss it to the light of God by saying a protection prayer and ending communication immediately.*

3. Tell me about Jesus Christ and God. *This is a very important question, if there is anything negative said to you or it blasphemes the name of Christ, this is a strong indicator you have connected to a lower entity and you should dismiss it to the light of God by saying a protection prayer and ending communication immediately. If they answer positively go onto the next questions.*

4. How do we know each other? What is our association? Have you had previous human incarnations?

5. Are you my primary life guide in this lifetime?

6. Who is(are) my primary guide(s), angel(s) and archangel?

7. What is the next action step I should take to bring more peace and healing into my life?

8. What wisdom do you have to share with me today?

Exercises to Help Open Your Psychic Awareness and Sensitivity Further

Refer to the book *BE A MASTER® of Psychic Energy* for many examples and exercises that can help you grow your clairvoyant abilities, so you may be more open to the channeling process. I find it easier to channel when you're in the space of unconditional love. Holding a pet, thinking of a loved one that passed, listening to beautiful music or anything that gets you into the high frequency of connection will make the process much easier.

Be 'Pure Love' For a Full 12 Hours Exercise

Try to love everything and everyone for a full 12 hours from the time you wake up to the time you go to bed. Look at all people, events and thoughts, asking yourself, "What is good about this person, event or idea?" even if someone was rude and just flipped you off after cutting you off on the highway, forgive and love them. If you feel a negative thought or judgement about someone you must rewrite that thought immediately by thinking and saying, "Delete, Rewrite." Then, rephrase the negative into a positive and go on with a smile on your face. You must keep doing this exercise until you can go through a whole day being 'pure love'. This is a very challenging thing to do at first, however, with time, the idea is to switch your energy field so that you attract more good into your reality, thus opening you up to communication with your guides at a deeper level. You must 'become love' to connect to higher vibratory beings.

Standing Mirror Exercise

This exercise is mentioned in *BE A MASTER® of Psychic Energy*, though I felt it is important to mention here as well because of its significance to fully loving self. Stand close to a full-length mirror. Look at your face; then focus in on your eyes. See your joyful loving inner child while you look in the mirror. Take your mind to a very young age before any trauma, when you were 100 percent pure love and light, freshly delivered from the other side – our eternal home. To this you must connect again. That's the energy that will open up your channeling abilities. If you need help, review photos and videos of yourself as a child. After you do this exercise for a while you can graduate to part two. Stand nude in front of a full-length mirror. Love all of you, as is - without judgement. Learning to love your mind, body and spirit, this will greatly open your channeling ability.

Dream Analysis Exercise

Another important exercise in helping you connect with messages from Spirit is dream analysis. Prior to falling asleep, place your pen and dream journal by your night stand. Say a prayer requesting that you remember your dreams when you awaken. Ask for messages of meaning from your higher self, angels and life guides. Upon waking, immediately write it all down in the dream journal so you can research online others' similar dream images on dream analysis websites to see what the images meant. Your guides and angels speak through pictures and emotions. During the dream state, we "let go" and lighten ourselves easily so our guides can speak to us without the heavy human filters we hold in our waking state. The images you see and remember have meanings you can look up through dream analysis. The dreams fade quickly however once you wake up, as the more you give focus to your life agenda in the waking state, the faster the dream information from the other side is forgotten or 'erased'. For more information on focus, intent, dreams and creating your own sleep study, read *BE A MASTER® of Psychic Energy.*

Personal Tips for Connecting with Spirit

- Spiritual work uses all the mental, emotional and physical tools humans have in their current lifetime to hyperdrive them into matching their guide's higher frequency. Along with a relaxed happy state, proper nutrition and hydration is essential. Avoid body and mind fatigue by eating about one-and-a-half hours prior to your session, though do not overeat as that can slow you down. You want to have just enough glucose in the blood to power you through your session. Your body's recourses should not be concentrated in digesting food from a heavy meal, but instead be readily available for channeling. For more nutritional high energy foods and preparation for reading sessions, refer again to my previous book, *BE A MASTER® of Psychic Energy.*

- Sitting still in a comfortable position and removing the mind's concern with the body is important as channeling sessions are typically long depending on the depth of connection and message involved. I enjoy a seated position usually in an office chair with lumbar support. I also have one of two pillows I position on my lap or under my forearms for support as needed. I sit with my spine as straight as possible and then pad myself accordingly to maintain this position even if my body starts to slump during a session. If this does happen, my guide or higher self usually readjusts me automatically if discomfit occurs to me and it starts to hinder our communication. If the room temperature is low, I will also have a light blanket over my hands and feet to keep me warm through the session. I find the more comfortable the body is, the less my body fidgets around and this allows my connection to improve. Movement is natural when you are channeling, some light rocking back and forth or fidgeting is usual, as the body stays grounded. Overly theatrical yelling and moving about – or uncomfortable sensations that seem to bother the channel are always 'suspect'. A loving spirit will not upset the body's harmony to the point that it brings harm to the channel.

- I always say a prayer prior to the session and end with gratitude afterwards. Set your intention and ask the love and light of God's Divine sources to clear the room and healing space of any lower vibrations so that the energy involved is of the highest possible level. If the invitation, intention and prayer is not set prior to a session, you are risking invitation of random unpleasant thoughts and energies from the day, picked up from others or unrelated issues, to corrupt the session's true nature. These energies may be incorporated in the flow, thus tainting and contaminating the space. The clearer and closer to a loving intention all parties involved are, the higher the connection. When the light is present, no darkness can remain.

Chapter Six: The Process of Channeling

"Channeling is your higher-self streaming through in a version your limited mind can accept. There is no such thing as a separate entity, only the perception of it. You are all of it!
~ Erin Fall Haskell

Channeling Spirit is an easy process but has become very complicated to understand due to the confusion put between your physical self and your higher self. Bombardment of religious groups' and government-controlled agendas, thoughts and desires of mass media to persuade a blind herd through social media, radio, television, magazines, and other means have overstimulated and filled our minds to mush with unimportant things. How many times could you not get a song out of your mind that you heard on a morning ride to work which served no purpose to your higher good? How many images of terror are stuck in your mind from all those horror movies you watched as a child, which paralyze you unknowingly now as an adult? How many bad habits and desires were imprinted into you from childhood by adults though traumatic experiences in the home? Obese parents eating poorly which can trigger disease continues the cycle in the children who think junk foods are acceptable nutrition, making it difficult for the child, who is now an adult, to regulate his or her healthy blood levels so as not to activate diseases like diabetes. Useless laws make mind-enhancing herbs illegal and discourage their use and block deep spiritual expansion which was allowed by ancient civilizations. Addition of fluoride into the water systems calcifies the pineal gland and blocks higher mind activity. The system encourages pharmaceutical drug use to numb and cover symptoms, caffeine and fast food to keep the body working, creating a 'superficial fix' go-go-go society. Multiply these negative things a thousand-fold over decades into older adulthood. Meditation and prayer to clear the mind and soul from the loaded, overwhelming world, are not properly taught in our school system. This is why we have the current situation in the Western world. To combat this mental fog, we turn to a deep meditation at some point in our day as adults trying to combat the "stress debt" we accumulated.

The idea of being connected to God just during meditation however, is a linear thought because connection to spirit is actually a 24/7 - 365-day idea, not a part-time activity that is done between work and time at the gym. How does one cultivate a connection that may have been there at one point, especially during childhood - when innocence, joy and love ruled the day? How can we quiet the mind and at the same time invite a strong download of information to manifest so that we can develop our psychic link?

Auto Writing Helps Open the Way

The automatic writing process helps widen our belief systems for more trust and greater connection with spirit. I'm a big believer in the automatic writing process as this is how I started to connect deeper with spirit. Outside of the usual book organizational editing process and gathering of my experiences, transcripts and personal notes, this book is channeled material from my higher self and 'unseen friends' or guides. As a matter of fact, all my books have been started through auto writing once I started to type or write, wonderful information started to flow in. You must understand, I was never a fan of writing any full-page essay in grade school or ten-page term paper in high school. Telling me I would be an author of several books in my later years, was simply unimaginable; I would have never believed you. Yet here we are, many books later and I still enjoy the process. I put a pen to a paper or my fingers over the computer keyboard and I let my mind 'go play' as the information flows. The gems were always there in my higher mind, I just had to find out how to download them to this reality. You too have valuable gifts, information, talents and visions ready to come forth. It is my desire to help those I meet in my seminars or in the clinic to open this flow, and to help them harness their immense personal power through the Kousouli® Method.

Simply sit quietly after meditation and prayer as mentioned in the steps for automatic writing in *BE A MASTER® of Psychic Energy*. Repetition of wisdom and wording unfamiliar to the conscious mind of the writer will confirm to them that it's a real phenomenon. At first, it feels as if you are making it up, but so what? Just let your imagination run with it. It will show you that you are not making it up; it is a process that will unfold as the language and information you read later will astound you.

An example follows of information coming from an unseen friend through automatic writing after a deep meditation to my mental question: "What is going on, I have been feeling depleted lately, am I okay? I feel very tired and foggy in my connection, why?" After about a minute of focusing, my mind and hand synced with my life guide and I felt a female energy who I later found out was named Ariadne, one of my four life guides, speaking to me as the following message came through my hand to the paper:

"Let the body heal – all is well – rest as needed. Spend time with me. I am here, always. Have patience with the process, just be. Yes, pray more, trust more. Pay attention better. Don't stop. So much love here for you. Yes, I am real. Here to help you transition as a healer to your next step, for the work you will be doing."

Ariadne projected an image of herself as a beautiful empress-like being, and the name 'Ariadne' was confirmed by intuitive medium Marisa Marinos two weeks later when I also saw Jesus as being part of my higher self in a vision.

"All is well. Meditate more. Take time for your body. Let go of the idea that you are not loved and are alone. Let go of the doubt, the fear. Come open. I stand side by side with you. Align. I am with you, I will send you more examples of symmetry. When they occur, stop, ask and listen, to build our connection. Look at the videos and photos of you as a child. Look into your eyes in the video. We love you."

I was elated with joy after I received that message, and then I asked a follow up question, "What is troubling my spiritual growth at this time?" The same voice spoke within my mind as my hand wrote the following:

"Fear and ridicule, the fear of not fitting in is blocking you. Choose to step out into non-conformity. You're sensitive for good reason. Don't stay hindered. it blocks the love you're able to give and receive. Be open, no one can harm you; you will accomplish much more than you have done. The amount and speed will depend on this. Be open and see what happens. Glory to God. Let go of procrastination, let go of what others think of you, follow your heart. Let go of the old as a snake sheds its dead skin. You cannot please all people all the time, channel for yourself, for your divine spiritual order. It is as simple as being done. Choices. God gives you all you ask for. It is up to you to follow through with action. Comfort kills creativity and forward movement. Remember what you already know. Stop being concerned with how it all will be brought to you, it just will be. Trust what is inevitably shown to you and fully believe."

Information Goes Back and Forth Between Our Realities

So how did I receive the previous information on a piece of paper after I connected, and my hand started to write? Think of a tennis analogy. Your unseen friend on the other side of the net is living in a reality different from our reality and we live in one that is different from theirs. We meet in the middle by raising, lightening and quickening, our vibration, and they lower theirs by slowing down and deepening their vibration, so that we intersect. We are on the same court, separated by a net. The net has holes and the ball (the information) goes back and forth over the net. Sometimes it gets caught in the net (in our case, that is resistance, bias, doubt or some other human filter). When in proper play, the ball is in motion being received and sent by both.

The info can come as a packet that can flow onto paper, as does automatic writing, or through sounds from the vocal cords as in vocal channeling.

Before I was able to become a vocal channel, I had to change certain beliefs within myself while strengthening others that served me.

Realizations I Had to Hold as My New 'Truth' to Be a Clear Channel

Prior to being able to dive deeper into my journey of channeling, I had to let go of any beliefs that limited me in terms of connecting 'deeper'. My channeling mentor, Shawn Randall, helped her class restructure certain beliefs with these key phrases. Repeat these phrases to yourself to break false beliefs that keep you from connecting to your own guides and angels.

- I create my own reality.

- I can also be connected to my divine unseen friend(s).

- I am a lovable and deserving soul; I am not born into damnation. My Creator loves me. I love my Creator. Everyone learns from their 'sins' and challenges. My Creator is forever and always forgiving of my shortcomings as a human. It is man who condemns; not God.

- Unseen friends exist in their reality, as I exist in mine. If I open my mind to the unseen, the unseen will be seen. The unknown will be known.

- Reality of my unseen friends can connect to my reality and vice versa. They grow from our experience, as do I. We all exist in a co-creative multiverse.

- I have the ability to connect to my higher self anytime I wish. I am never without help. All I have to do is ask, listen and await the response.

- I know and believe in the value of channeling for myself and others.

- I don't have to be at any level to do channeling. I can start now.

- I am first spirit and secondly human. I am able to suspend all 'things' human.

- I am ALWAYS connected to my Guides, Angels, Archangels, God and the Divine. Channeling allows me to realize my connection's existence more often.

- Channeling makes my life better all the time. I am never alone. I am always guided and protected in my journey here.

- I believe in the evolution of consciousness and channeling.

- I take any emotions I feel for myself or others, which are lesser than love, and put them aside before channeling. I diffuse all lesser vibrations with love.

- Channeling is not a control process. It's a co-creation flow, that needs me to let go of ego and let God work through me. I allow more of what I already am – God's flow and my light force.

- How long it takes me to channel will be as long as it takes me to let go of my static resistance (fears, anxiety, shame, worthlessness and worries).

- Everyone has a uniquely different path to opening up their access to their unseen friends. I have my own pace and path, and that's perfectly fine with me. I don't need to compare my uniqueness with anyone else's.

- My dedication to the process is needed to build trust both ways. I understand time dedicated in deep meditation is a part of the process.

- I love myself confidently in a healthy way, in all ways.

- If I ever feel powerless in my life, it is because I've allowed it by choosing to focus my attention on something other than my powerful connection with God.

How to Channel for Yourself

All people have their own way of channeling their guides, as it becomes a process unique to the individual. However, there is a general process; I explain that process and how I do it starting with my affirmation invocation. You will of course, develop your own way to channel and may use your own prayer. After quieting your mind and completing a deep meditation, as explained in *BE A MASTER® of Psychic Energy;* have closed your eyes and are sitting in silence in a meditative position, pay attention to whispers or images that enter your mind.

Step 1. Always begin a channel session with an affirmation invocation (Invitation and prayer) that states your intention and calls over your spirit guides. The one I personally use is:

"By the power of our Original Creator in Christ Consciousness, I now invite

only my life guides, angels and archangels of highest good to speak clearly through me and to me with wisdom, truth, love and compassion. Any energies lesser than love are directed to the light. (In Greek- εἰς τὸ ὄνομα τοῦ Πατρὸς καὶ τοῦ Υἱοῦ καὶ τοῦ Ἁγίου Πνεύματος) In the name of the Father, Son and Holy Spirit, Amen."

Step 2. Meditate, quiet the mind completely and become completely relaxed. Let go of all your human attachments, bias, and the day's stressful emotions. Flood your heart and mind with immense child-like joy. Let peace come in through you inside and out.

Step 3. Allow your conscious mind to step aside to permit a trance-like state to let messages come through. Envision in your mind's eye that you are leaving for a small trip, packing your suitcase and leaving out the back door. Your house sitter enters and comfortably settles in. **Allow your unseen friend(s) to appear to you.** Visualize your higher mind bringing them forward to you. If you need to see yourself in a beautiful field or meadow as a meeting spot, feel their presence with a light loving energy associated with their presence. Mentally ask your question and await the subtle answer. **Listen** with patience, even if it takes a few minutes in silence, and **receive**. Concentrate on allowing the information flow and freely permit the information to stream in, trusting what you are receiving without doubting. Allow the information you are receiving to be vocalized. **Speak what you feel, hear, or see in your mind's eye without filtering or being critical** of the information. Let the flow go straight from the mind to the vocal cords (or the hand if auto writing). Don't worry if it sounds garbled or makes no sense at first. Over time this flow becomes faster and more concrete. Stay on the flow. Practice these steps often.

Congratulations, you're now vocally channeling. That's it. Simple.

"But Dr. Kousouli, I need more information, this doesn't do it for me!" Well, that's your human ego screaming: "I MUST complicate this simple process! It can't be that easy!" Guest what? Yes. It. Is. Your ego is the limiting factor.

Don't worry, I felt exactly the same way, thinking it had to be MUCH more complicated than this. However, it is not. The difficulty comes from our human perception, not from the higher-self. Once in a trance, you will start to pick up the queues from the spirit world; it's like learning a completely new language. A communication rapport needs to be built between you and your spirit guides. With time you will discern your unique language between each other. The more often you practice, you will be tuning your vibration to notice finer and finer communication from your spirit guides. There is no substitute to this process of practice. The more often you do this building of relationship, the faster and easier the process will become. Just as riding a bike, eventually you will be riding faster and fearlessly. However, in the beginning you will have several falls and scrapes as you build trust in your abilities and the communication of your unseen friends. DO NOT give up. Channeling takes perseverance and dedication through all the beginning frustrations to develop the skill. The learning curve is the first year of practice. In the coming chapters you will peek into my own personal intimate development which will help you also break into your personal connection with spirit.

You must have confidence. Build on your beliefs and trust that the process can work for you as well. Like on a surf board, at first you will slide off many times – but after time you will be flowing like a professional. Same goes with channeling. Continued experience will be the key in developing better spiritual communication. You can read all the instructional material possible on the process of spirit channeling, however nothing but experience and action in taking steps forward will override your human filters to experience a clear channeling process. Embrace the love and embrace the intimate personal process. How deep is your love for meeting your spirit guides and the higher version of you? Only you can answer this.

Main Reasons Most Don't Connect to a Benevolent Loving Spirit:

According to Shawn Randall, there are four main categories of **resistance** that can keep people from reaching the love of spirit communication to channel correctly. Many times, failure to thrive in life also stems from FEAR and is very much interrelated to these four categories. One may suffer from one or a mixture of all four. Without clearing these human filters, channeling of a benevolent loving guide will be hindered, as you won't be able to lift to their high level of communication.

1. Clinging to the past. Traumatic past life, old belief, subconscious issue from youth or current life's trauma story.

2. Toxic blame. Blaming self, others or something; a martyr or victim mentality blocks all receiving. *Playing the violin of sorrows.*

3. Self-pity. A false sense of self nurturing, usually from childhood. *Oh, poor me! Attitude. Repeating a drama story for sympathy.*

4. Lack of self-responsibility or willingness. Avoidance or self-empowerment, responsibility, owning it. *Laziness in not developing oneself spiritually.*

Differentiating 'Who' is Speaking

Shawn taught us to simply ask the energy to identify itself. Who is speaking to me right now? Who is here with us? The unseen friend may refer to itself as 'We' meaning there are more than one present, a group or a collective force. Guides and teachers from the light and love will have a fun and loving personality. Unseen friends who have your highest good intentions will not tell you what to do but will recommend healthy options for you to become aware of on the journey of life.

The higher self may also speak to you. When it does it may use 'I' with a denser feeling, possibly also very stern in its' advice to you. Some describe this as a feeling of 'God's voice' vibrating deeply, sternly and powerfully throughout and within the air in all of one's surroundings.

How to Know Messages are Coming from Love and Light

In her channeling class, Shawn Randall explained to us that from the spirit's perspective, they will use our imagination, language and personal culture, or 'the tool kit' of each person, to communicate their message. Experience and accuracy comes with building the bridge with repetitive practice. The path is different and unique for all. Steps are general, practice with patience is vital. As you develop rapport with unseen entities, these seven questions will help you distinguish if the energies have good or bad intentions for you.

Shawn advised we always ask ourselves these important questions during each encounter:

1. Is the information I am receiving useful to my life? *Can the information make me better?*

2. Does it uplift my spirit and bring joy? *Is it said lovingly? Compassionately?*

3. Does it assist my spiritual growth? *Does it make sense as the next logical step for me to take?*

4. Is this information blaming or shaming me? *Is it critical of me or does it put me down in any way? Is it a parental projection?*

5. Is it grandiosity of self? Ask: Does it feed my ego? *Am I being told I am 'special' compared to others and I should feel superior?*

6. Does this harm, manipulate or trick me in any way? *Am I being led to harm myself or others physically?*

7. Do I feel I need to be right or prove something? *Am I being led to make others feel bad so I can feel good?*

If EGO interrupts the positive 'yes' flow to the above questions, you may be allowing too much of the human filter or bias to affect the information, or the energies you have connected to are not of the highest love and light vibration.

Moving Through the Difficulties of Energy Fog

A good indication one is in a 'fog' or frustrated with becoming more aware in spirit, is a blanket of emotions that seem to follow them in their life: anger, rage, regret, indecisiveness, doubt, hate, fear and jealousy. If you feel sad, depressed, tired or angry you will attract bad vibes. When you start to channel you will surely become much more sensitive. Feelings, ideas, and emotions will be felt much more strongly when you start to open multi-dimensionally. Always lean towards the good vibes.

If you think you're receiving energies that aren't of the highest good intention, immediately send them to the light of God, and stop further communication. For more information on dark forces and removing negativity from one's life read *BE A MASTER® of Psychic Energy*.

Wisdom from Beyond

The following are messages from Heroditus, my main healer guide as of the time of this publication. For a long time, I felt an energy present when healings occurred, and as you will read later from our communications, he identified himself as well as the identities of my four main life guides. The following is an excerpt of the first few channeling sessions where Heroditus came through me vocally in Shawn Randall's channeling class to share his wisdom.

Thursday September 15, 2017
9pm in Shawn Randall's Channeling Class

After completing the affirmation invocation process; I channeled Heroditus, answering questions on soul mates and our child essence.

Student: Can you tell me about soul mates?
Heroditus: General or specifics?
Student: Can we do both?
Heroditus: Certainly!
Student: Is the soul mate for a season, a reason or a lifetime?
Heroditus: All of the above. Soulmates are energies of your own that appear to be separate in this lifetime. They are on this earth because you have preplanned - to meet that other version of your 'self' - of your own divinity - so that you can enjoy contrast for your mutual growth. This is so that God can re-learn of Himself, Herself, Itself, from many different angles, to re-upload to the ALL on the conclusion of each physical lifetime here. This is going on in a consistent basis all over the multiverse, galaxies, for many many trillions of beings – always. So, the concept of soul mate is a concept of reconnection of yourself to yourself however in this phenomenon - in this reality on this earth - you enjoy them as another being. So, when you do meet that other being, you have a fond familiarity with that being and you do claim: "Oh I feel as if I have known you forever!" and indeed this is the case, you have known yourself forever! (Laughter) It is a beautiful thing when this awareness occurs, however many people know that with soulmates - over a period of time - a disconnection may occur, or a similarity ends and then the problems or challenges that must be overcome surface. This doesn't mean the person is no longer a soul mate; they are indeed a soul mate. But what does soul mate mean? Exactly that - a mate for your soul. This is again my original explanation, you teaching you something.
Student: Yes.
Heroditus: Isn't this interesting?

Student: Mmm hmm!

Heroditus: Most people think this is a 'lovey-dovey' feeling all the time. It is only when that version of yourself is coming to terms with that time of your life where you have to meet that type of love vibration. A twin flame is a soul mate that is for the purposes of deep passionate love and what your 'Hollywood' has stereotyped as a happily ever after relationship scenario as in the movies. However, this version is not the case for everyone all the time. There are some lifetimes you have indeed had this type of interaction occur, and there are lifetimes it didn't, and you chose to learn other lessons and have other experiences. It is ideal to change and grow - that is your purpose here and soulmates remind you of this.

Student: Yes, there is sadness that occurs though in that too. It's so heavy on the heart.

Heroditus: True it is sad, but that is the rainbow of the emotions that the human being must - and loves - to experience from our side and point of view. When I was incarnate I had all those feelings, and now seeing from the point of view here, I tell you there is no sorrow on our side, only the meaning you give it on your side. There is nothing but joy, beauty – the All - How can you feel the depths of despair when all you know is the truth? The truth - is -Love. You cannot know the opposite. That is why you come to Earth, to this or other worlds - to enjoy being - and to enjoy the contrast, as the channel likes to say, "No one wants pasta every night - forever," which means, you have to spice up the pasta with different herbs, but eventually you will be tired of the pasta. However, since you really like pasta - eventually you will return to it. So, after this lifetime loved one, you will recreate everything from the beginning, and you will start painting your picture. If you choose to bring in a soul mate for various new growth, you can. If you wish to enjoy a romance with a new twin flame, in the next lifetime you can - it is all available to you. The choices you make in this lifetime are for your growth and will continue to be for your growth, however the idea that everyone in this lifetime must find their twin flame is a fairytale, for there will be little to no growth if every time you came into a new world you were with the same lover twin flame. You will say, I no

longer want pasta. (Laughter) Indeed this would be the scenario.
Student: If you outgrew the pasta?
Heroditus: Yes, you may want it and you will have it - but pasta at some point won't fulfill the taste bud's need for a new adventure! You will leave it and find something more delish - another dish! Leave it - come back - leave it - and come back. You can do anything you like. Soul mates, yes - yes, but if we can expand on the concept of soulmates for you…
Student: Yes, please expand!
Heroditus: Everyone is a soulmate! Everyone. They are all offering teachings. Even the person who stabs you in the back, or the one who killed you in a past lifetime. The person who lies to your face is a potential soul mate! Now, astrologically and numerologically speaking, the ones who match up - yes, that is a definite soulmate, there is a lesson there.
Student: Yes! You hit the pay dirt there, which was my question, you answered as I was thinking it, thank you.
Heroditus: You are very welcome.
Another student asks: Heroditus, can you tell us about the inner child and aging?
Heroditus: You are always the child when you wish to connect to the child. You never stopped being the child in another dimensional space or alternate reality. For example, the channel, Theodore, has only formed a new consciousness of ideas and thoughts that have shaped the sub-atomic molecular structure to be that of a 40-year-old man at this time in 'reality'. So, he sees before him a version that suits his needs at this time in experiencing his journey. He has mastered the 39 years prior. You all are doing this. When you graduate or master an understanding that no longer serves you, you will move onto another that does. Aging in a sense is the expectation of ideas learned from your parents and seniors of what you can expect as you gain more experience. You contort the atoms projected into physical viewing by your mind every time you exclaim "Happy Birthday," you take on the idea you are getting older. We recommend to you that you may want to slow this process down. You can slow it down and sometimes reverse the process for a period of time. However, you won't be able to stop

it completely at this time of your earth consciousness, for to stop it may inhibit your idea of forward growth progress. You want to experience the development as a child before you can take on the challenges of a young adult. When finished with those lessons, you move into creating your adult version with all the benefits of experience that came from the earlier free-will choices you made. Your soul thrives on experiences and enjoying each and every lesson. This serves you until the physical body no longer serves the soul's purpose in that life period. When it has run its course, and the preplanned agreement to fulfill its duties - or not, is finished, the physical body is shed and your consciousness moves on to create another version of itself. The ego sometimes does not wish to change the outward look of the body and you see that often with the plastic surgeries to maintain a youthful look. However, many times if the individual is not in line with their joy and aligned only with their ego, the results may not be as glorious as they hoped they would be. The child-like essence however is always there. A state of meditation as you all know, allows you to tap into this. Through this connection you can experience that, exactly what you are as a soul. Joy is continuously available to you for that is what you are originally at your core origins - made from love! Your external presence is a manifestation of your consciousness loved ones. The channel, would not be taken seriously by any peers if he wore scrubs and proclaimed he was a doctor with high accolades at ten or twenty years old. Same as he would not be taken seriously if asked his age and he told them he is five years old. There is also a very real co-creative aspect to your physical nature. When the lessons are learned per day, week and year, the consciousness forms the physical body as a reflection of all the consciousnesses. I suggest this - You have photos in your realm of various ages you felt happy and healthy. Take this photo of when you felt youthful and happy. Put this in your billfold, on your computer monitor, desk, and every time you look at it. Smile and say to yourself. "This is me." Your cells will hear you and start to behave appropriately. Over time, you will feel the positive changes. This I guarantee. With love I depart, we will talk again soon - Heroditus.

Thursday, September 28th, 2017
9:45 PM Shawn Randall's Channeling Class

After completing the affirmation invocation process; I channeled Heroditus for students on the topic of letting go.

Heroditus: Greetings loved ones, I am Heroditus.
Student: Heroditus, please tell us about letting go of the things that bother us. Pet peeves for instance.
Heroditus: A perfect discussion for tonight. You are always working through your perfect imperfections. And are they not such? They're the little nuisances that bother you and cause a reaction instead of proactive solution. Sometimes we like to help remind the channel, whether it be through the stress endured sitting in traffic, or someone stalling him by walking slowly in front of him and blocking his progress while he is trying to get somewhere, that in this moment he is confronting his confrontation. Look deeper into the subconscious offense that you believe is hurting you. It is a lie. It is a belief created within you to have an excuse to react to unfinished business because the issue was not correctly solved at an earlier time; ex - such as a childhood trauma. When you have the inability to speak out - your soul yearns to open up under distress of created events. Using your power of heart and mind to speak your truth in this world, you compensate the throat chakra's function. And you compensate to develop a matrix of lessons to be learned. A perfect matrix created by you for you. All your challenges now and in the future are created by you - from a higher level of understanding and creation. You are co-creator. When you come to understand these things from this higher co-creative mind, nothing will take you off your course of joy. You may burn your toast - but you will also learn that you can enjoy it. Understand that in everything that happens from now forward, for the channel knows huge contrast to a 'good day'. When he had open heart surgeries to look forward to and prepare for - twice - and then heal from both, that was set by him for him. With us by his side, we have helped him see the brighter side of things. He does stop

and think now about the events before him proactively, rather than being reactive. He hadn't done this in the past. When turmoil struck, he would be consumed by the events; emotions overtook him. He was much less able to cope and sat in his despair much longer. All of you in your lives also, fellow soul seekers - were less able to handle the stresses that came, you did not look deeply inside, but rather used superficial means to match the energies coming at you. You did this over and over again, hitting your heads over the proverbial wall until you saw this as no longer working or serving you. Instead, you found the power of meditation and went deep into yourselves with fellow travelers in classes like these, at a time where it suited you best. For you came to an awareness and understanding that you would like to lead by example in some way, shape or form – whether it is your friends, family, or masses such as the channel is preparing for, and you asked the important questions. So, these little things that bother you are actually big things that allow you greater understanding day by day, so that one day you look back a year or two from now and say, "wow, nothing bothers me anymore. I can create with others in solidarity and love. All my relationships, I understand them," and is this not the perfect imperfection you all seek? For you cannot be 100 percent perfect here, though you are seen as such from our side. You are to us, as we are to you. In many ways we are also continually developing, continuously growing, working with you and other souls and other forms on other planets, we are growing, you are growing, the Universe is growing, God is growing. All is good all is well, and with this I thank you. I depart, love to you all - Heroditus.

Thursday, October 12, 2017, at 9:45 PM in Shawn Randall's Channeling Class

After completing the affirmation invocation process; I channeled Heroditus for students on the topic of miracles.

Heroditus: Greetings loved ones, I am Heroditus.
Student: Heroditus, can you tell us about miracles?

Heroditus: Yes, miracles. There are currently six in the room facing one another. You are all looking at miracles. The chances of you even existing in that body is a miracle in itself. The joining and union of sperm and egg is a miracle. How quickly one forgets this. How many on Earth cause hurt and pain to one another without compassion, without empathy in their hearts. They forget who they harm; a fellow miracle - a projection of themselves. Another human who they attack in spite, as in the act of cursing, punching, maiming or any kind of malicious gesture is done in actuality, to oneself. All of it, good or bad turns to be the lesson in disguise. Respect all as miracles. You are all miracles. If you can remember this, the miracle will become the norm, not the rarity. The human currently does not expect to see miracles. However, classes like these and the individuals waking up to the new found human potential, can do and are, through the power of the Creator - within self, awaken to miracles. You, my brothers and sisters, will see more miracles and more miracles. This in itself will be the new norm. This is coming for you all. Specifically, the group in this room. You are not strangers to miracles. Your belief in them is the first step to seeing them. Just as when you purchase a new red car, it is a spontaneous miracle you so often notice other red cars around your periphery. So, let us make it instead of a red car, let's just say miracles for all, all the time, in every way for everyone. The miracle continues to give, continues to gift itself over and over. Love and humility for yourself and one another spark the fire of the miracle, a truly beautiful event, spontaneous, unbound love that lacks all ego. With much love, until next time - Heroditus.

Thursday, October 19, 2017
9:33 PM in Shawn Randall's Channeling Class

After completing the affirmation invocation process; I channeled Heroditus for students on the topic of the death and the challenges that people are facing as they go through Hurricane Harvey.

Heroditus: Greetings loved ones - I am Heroditus.

Student: Heroditus, please tell us about death and why the current natural disaster Hurricane Harvey is happening to all those people?

Heroditus: So, I ask of you, Am I alive or am I dead? You spoke of the passing of a prominent spiritual figure in class today, and I ask you, is this spirit alive to us and dead to you? An interesting notion to ponder. As there is no 'reality' in death and it has no sting. As you have come to understand in your personal lessons and quest, I am here to give you tonight more insight to the knowledge and perception of death. Humanity still struggles with the concept of death. Death on your planet is a goodbye from the ego. The ego is the only part that hurts when a transition occurs from physical reality to spiritual reality; from your 'five senses' realm to our unlimited realm. The ego is at a loss for not seeing, touching or interacting with the loved one via the physical senses. The loss is perceived as a massive change which the ego does want to occur without its permission. So, I ask again, as I am not with a physical body, "Am I alive or am I dead to you?" I would very much say we are all alive. You are as much alive as I am; I just have a different perception than you do, being you have come to this planet to express yourselves in a limited capacity within these bodies, cramming yourselves into these beautiful forms of Godly creation - so that you can take, as the channel likes to say, "The 'We' stuffed into the 'Me'." This allowed you to check your grand individuality from a limited aspect, re-creating yourselves to experience the awe of life once again. This is the perception you must look at in your lives and the lives of those going through a perceived disaster. They are blessed just as you are, even though you may be here in comfortable seats in California while they are going through a massive uncomfortable change - that yes, they have chosen to go through in an unknown way to them in this world. Unknown to them in their conscious mind, but their higher-self was okay with this arrangement for they knew they would use the event(s) to transition into a new life there or in the next. All is blessed, all is good, all is in God. There is no pain in reality, only the perception of it, and what the soul chooses to go through to graduate. I have chosen not to re-incarnate at this time to help the channel, while he has chosen to incarnate. This is our unity, our agreement. I may later decide to reincarnate with him at the same time, or he may choose to help me from this side of the veil while I seek his guidance as I create my life as a human being. All is blessed, all is good, all is in God. We love you immensely; in every moment of your existence. You are with us all the time; we are with you in all the moments: In every heartbeat, every breath, in every molecule of your being. We are the speck of sand, we are the Universe, we are the portal. With much love for all of you, your choices and decisions, the mass consciousness you create on a daily basis, much love to all of you, until we meet again, - Heroditus.

Chapter Seven: Communicating Between Worlds

"Excess of grief for the dead is madness, for it is an injury to the living, and the dead know it not."
~ Xenophon

Beginners on their spiritual journey often get confused between the meaning of psychic, empath, intuitive, channel, and medium. I have previously explained the definitions of psychic, intuition and empath in my previous work, *BE A MASTER® of Psychic Energy*, so in this chapter I will specifically shed more light on mediumship and its role in serving through channeling.

According to Merriam-Webster's dictionary, the word medium is defined as "go-between, intermediary; an individual held to be a channel of communication between the earthly world and a world of spirits."
Channels are conduits of the cosmic flow, life guides, master teachers and Divine insight, while mediums are conduits for connecting to your dead cousin Vinny.

To explain further, mediums are channels who have the unique gift of communicating with the deceased who have crossed over, have dropped their physical form and are now considered discarnate spirits. Mediums serve in many ways. Many help detectives solve crimes and fill in missing leads that have gone cold on cases. Others help grieving mothers heal by helping them understand why their child left so early, and others give guidance and personal assistance in private to officials and heads of state to help them make big decisions.

Many times, these sensitive humans haven't closed off the gift they received in childhood and have learned to trust the 'voices in their minds' since childhood. When many of us were told that our special friends who played with us or drank tea with us were imaginary, mediums chose to stick with what they knew was true and kept that connection open.

Los Angeles intuitive medium, Marisa Marinos, who helps many connect with their deceased loved ones explains, "The voices that speak to you - are your personal GPS. When you tune in and really listen, they will lead you to a completely different space. Trust your GPS - it's a gift."

When a medium directly communicates with the deceased, they are directly working with the discarnate energies. Through channeled mediumship, a vocal channel can also serve as a medium.

Channeled mediumship as explained in this book is the process of using one's life guides to filter energies on the other side before being allowed to participate in the communication. The life guides then relay the information from the discarnate to those seeking to connect to the discarnate, usually a family member or loved one. Your life guide functions as a 'bouncer' letting through only the non-physical energies who are well intended and meant to step forward for connection. This connection is also much easier on the channel, for taking on discarnate energies on their own can lead to very deep swings of emotion, mood and be physically draining on overall health.

Spirit Connects for Higher Purpose

A shared purpose, unfinished business or gratitude with intense love brings Divine guidance from the spirit world to communicate with you. Grief, anger and fear blocks the connection of speaking with those who have passed over. I shared a very loving connection with my Uncle Tony when he was here with me physically on earth. I missed him so much when he passed and recollect his humor and light-hearted, child-like playfulness when we joked at the family restaurant. I would feel love for him still talking out to him, laughing while remembering fun times, just as if he was still with me here in physical form. I felt he still heard me and we were still very much in touch. This continued for some years until I further sought to develop my psychic training, and when I was ready, Uncle Tony opened up my communication also to my life and healer guides who I didn't consciously know or ever met in this lifetime.

Focus on the Messengers' Messages, not the Horse They Rode in on

Meditation and coherence with a high-energy prayer will connect to the beings, or 'unseen friends'. Similar mindset is important to have before starting communication. Think of connection to spirit as using a tool to reach an objective. Channeling is the tool as the message which enriches your life is the objective. Likewise, the phone is the tool used to speak to a loved one and the message of connection and love is the end objective. Do not get dependent on a spirit board, EVP, tarot, crystals, or any 'item' to fascinate on sensationalize yourself with spirit. You don't fall in love with the phone, text message or email, but rather focus on the message that you receive that helps you grow soulfully. It is very dangerous to put your reassurance and trust into anything other than the useful loving message itself because that can bring about a loss of power and disempowerment, and this is not what spiritual connection is about. Disempowerment leads quickly to allowing nearby 'trickster' or lower energy vibrations to bring the sessions to an unhealthy place. Override this by having a deep desire to grow and improve upon your soul which helps bring loving energies to your awareness.

All kinds of people around the globe have benefitted by receiving information from the Other Side. Some use mediumship and channeling, gaining help from others who specialize in connection with the spirit world through other means, including telepathy and infused knowledge (which is just a knowing without understanding why). We all have the power to do these things ourselves, as I have continuously stated throughout this book. Examples abound of how connections with the Other Side can help the living. Sometimes, a person fears a departed loved one suffered greatly at his or her death. In cases like this, a medium or channel can ease the pain for the living by asking the departed direct questions.

Statements like, "Tell my Dad I left my body before the accident and didn't feel the crash," can do more for a parent than years of psychotherapy.

Every reading must contain some sort of a message, even if it's just, "Tell Johnny I love him." The message is the reason for the reading. Whether a person wants to find a valuable lost object or the murderer of a loved one, connecting with spirit through channels and mediums can be of help; in fact, often those on the Other Side are just waiting to be asked.

Lost items are retrieved, fears removed, and creativity magnified when spirits are invited to help solve a problem. Connecting with the Other Side can make individuals who have been affected by a death more stable and grounded once they understand the connection process.

Detectives in some police departments and sheriff's offices use people who have developed their psychic gifts to solve crimes. Law enforcement officers who work this way often say they ask the medium or channel to begin by asking the spirit simple things that are easy to answer yet no one else would know. This alerts the living that the entity present is actually the creator of the message, and the medium or channel is just repeating the message.

Examples law enforcement may begin with are: Where were you born in your last life? What color was your hair? How tall were you? Can you describe the color of your favorite dog? At this point, if the spirit had a cat, and not a dog, there may be a pause until the question is rephrased. On the other hand, a playful spirit might just say something like, "My family knows I never took much to dogs. But Chatty- her full name was Chattitude you know- was blonde with an orange streak across her nose." Police departments and other law enforcement agencies who use psychics usually don't reveal their sources. While some may say that's because the information really wasn't obtained in such an "unlikely" manner, the true reason is the same one journalists don't tell their sources. Once sources are revealed, there is much less chance of ever getting them to come through for you again.

Detectives say some of the psychics they use look at photos; others go to the victim's home or location of a crime scene; while others use psychometry, which is the process by which energy vibrations are given from an object owned by someone.

Although not all law enforcement agencies are open to the use of psychics, many more are willing to work with them than just thirty years ago.

Being of More Service to Others

Once you are able to channel, are familiar with your life guides and angels and have built on the foundations of these relationships, you may be drawn to be of service to those who have lost loved ones through channeled mediumship. The amount of peace and healing that is received by the living yearning to connect with those who have passed on, cannot be described. Like I previously mentioned, the only limiting factor is you and your human ego self. As long as that is out of the way you will be amazed at what can happen for all involved. You may also want to review contents on how to do a reading in my previous book, *BE A MASTER® of Psychic Energy*, which will greatly help you understand the process of readings with spirit better.

The connection stories between my living clients and their departed loved ones is so very personal and intimate, that I have decided not to disclose transcripts of their interactions out of respect. However, in the next chapter I have revealed sensitive and personal information on how I grew my own spiritual connection. My intention in writing this book is to help you connect to your personal spiritual guides and protectors, ultimately bringing you closer to God. The best way I knew to do this was by sharing my own experience and the steps I took to connect deeply.

Even though I grew up in a very religious home solid in Eastern Orthodox teaching, it was not an easy path to knowing concretely that I have Divine guidance. It took me decades of time and a tremendous amount of adversity to get this far in my understanding. Some have it all figured out in their youth, some by middle age, and some sadly never find their connection at all. As I tried to make sense of the information shown to me in visions through the years, I sought out those who could help me 'unscramble' the screen. Only others who have traveled the path before, can open the door also for you.

Mentors can lovingly show you the way by opening the door, however you are the only one that must walk through the door. No one does that portion for you. No one but you. My pure desire to learn and the countless prayers asking to understand, led me to all my mentors; both in the healing arts and in spiritual subjects. Now, it's truly a much calmer and confident journey.

Personalized professional instruction and a determination to deeply connect makes the process flow much easier. Shawn Randall's loving instruction on channeling and the board work with my healer guide Heroditus done together in private, including the board work done with my light guide Tony and my sister (who was also going through a huge spiritual transformation at the time), have opened a wave of new growth potential. The information presented here will help you learn, just as I learned, about the channeling process and much, much more.

Chapter Eight: Wisdom from the Other Side

"We are spirits clad in veils." ~ Christopher Pearse Cranch

As I received the information from Source during each and every one of my auto writing, channeling or spirit board sessions, I immediately transcribed what came through onto paper and organized it into the book you are now reading.

After initially starting channeling class and to strengthen our link with our unseen friends, our instructor introduced us to the spirit board, a simple tool used by energy sensitives to contact their spirit guides. It consists of an approximately twelve-inch-tall by fourteen-inch-wide flat board made with letters and numbers on it and a smaller second piece; a small heart shaped planchette which the user(s) touch while guided by spirit to indicate or 'point' to a focused letter or number on the board to spell out a message. Now, obviously coming from a strong Christian background I had huge concerns using the Spirit Board. I had never used one prior; and I was glad I hadn't. My understanding of its proper use was so limited that if I had misused it, I may have been spooked by the process and created a negative association to its use by inviting unwanted forces, like many have done - to their spiritual detriment. However, I prayed and asked that if I was to connect with my guides and this was going to be a powerful boost in my belief system's expansion, then let God allow it. Being it was also shown to me by a trusted mentor which I was led to after praying, I knew I could trust the information coming forth and there was no need to put stock on the scary images of Hollywood's movie and Halloween horror folklore. I did plenty of research on the Spirit Board and found that it 'scientifically'

worked because of a strong subconscious desire to answer a question by the **ideomotor** or **'IMR' effect**. The ideomotor effect 'ideo' meaning idea and motor meaning movement, states that a subject makes reflexive motions unconsciously much like the idea of sucking on a lemon brings forth the secretory response. So, this is a 'built in' automatic function that humans can do but science doesn't fully understand, yet mystics term it a paranormal spiritual event. Great, now that seemed to make perfect logical sense and made it even more real to my 'scientific' mind...However, I wasn't taking any chances on science and its linear interpretation. I wanted to keep the communication clear with my own creative energy, so I designed my own personal board, not to taint its connection to my higher self. I did not want

to use a corporately mass -produced board that you can find in a store with various occult symbolism. This was too important, intimate and personal for me. I wanted the board to have the sign of Christ on it, the Orthodoxy IC XC NI KA crossed seal of God to ensure lower entities could not connect to it. I then printed it as I felt fit. For the planchette, I simply used an old audio CD and put some felt pads on it so it could slide on the board easily. As I constructed it, I felt my personal higher-mind energy creating the board, much like I instruct in creating an 'In-Vision' board for your life in my book *BE A MASTER® of Your Reality*; an important step in manifestation.

My level of understanding and communication with my spiritual advisers was about to go into skyrocketing mode. I was unaware of what was about to happen but had total faith and belief it was going to be a good experience. On Thursday Jan 12, 2017, everything I thought I knew expanded more than I could have ever imagined.

Note: Various inquiries were made into many subjects: prosperity, abundance, business and work, finding true love, dating, sexuality, recovering from a broken heart, dealing with stress, disease, removing negativity, miracles and healing, dealing with fear, space, aliens, tragic world events, the process of life and death, Heaven and Hell, spirituality, and many other topics that trouble the human mind. Everything you read is as it was communicated - raw - straight from Spirit. The names of participants have been changed to respect their privacy. At times conversations discussed move on to other topics abruptly, depending on the energy connection and focus at that time. Usual sessions were about an hour in length, however they greatly varied. Some discussed material may be sensitive to readers of contrasting belief structures, and that is acceptable as everyone processes information in their own way. These transcripts are only presented for understanding the process of Spirit communication and the growth that happens within.

Thursday, January 12, 2017 4:30 PM
Private board session. Dr. Theo at Shawn Randall's office. Teresa transcribes.

Shawn says her Affirmation/Invocation to start the session. My sister was present and witnessed everything. She wrote it all down as questions were being answered.

Shawn places her index, middle and ring fingertips from both hands lightly on the planchette of the board and I do the same. We are just lightly making contact, just enough finger pressure to feel the planchette under our fingertips.

My eyes widen in shock as the planchette starts to move to different letters and spell out words seemingly all by itself.

Unseen friend: Theo, hello. Finding you has been a pleasure! Finding our connection has been a joy. I am Heroditus.
Dr. Theo: Your name is Heroditus?
Heroditus: Oh yes.
Dr. Theo: In my meditations I was connecting to a female energy. You're not a female energy? (I later found out that was my life guide Ariadne)
Heroditus: Correct.
Dr. Theo: How do we know each other?
Heroditus: Greek clinics of yester-years.

Dr. Theo: Are you a Greek philosopher?
Heroditus: Yes. Teacher.
Dr. Theo: What did we do together?
Heroditus: Healers we were to wounded soldiers.
Dr. Theo: This feels right, but I'm just in total shock that we are clearly communicating and you say you know me. Can you please provide more details about our exact work together in the past?
Heroditus: When they returned from wards wounded in mind and body we soothed them first with conversation. Then we bathed them in white robes soaked in thyme and myrrh.
Dr. Theo: Am I now doing the same type of work as back then? I feel as if I do the same work with my mind/body healing technique.
Heroditus: Of course! Follow your instincts and go deeper into altered states to see where it leads you. You may discover dead medicines containing common easy compounds that heal in old - yet new - ways.
Dr. Theo: Please tell me how to help patients with the vitiligo de-pigmentation skin condition. It affects nearly 100 million people worldwide. What causes it?
Heroditus: Work with self-image issues of the patient. Wrap them in sheaths soaked in olive oil and herbs: Dear Theo research herbs.
Dr. Theo: Are you my primary guide?
Heroditus: One of them.
Dr. Theo: How many are there?
Heroditus: Depends on their function. I assist in your healing work, as do many others. Your 'life guides' number 4.
Dr. Theo: What are their names and the name of my primary Archangel?
Heroditus: Ariadne, Exter, Devous, and Joy are the 4. Archangel Gabriel sounds his horn for your protection and they all love you. Joy is wanting to speak through you - just for you personally, not clients.
Dr. Theo: What are some action steps I can take to take my healing practice to the world?
Heroditus: The world will come to you when you share more of it on social media and speak at expos. Books: update the older ones.

Dr. Theo: Heroditus, Why all the heart surgeries? I feel like I'm borrowing time every ten years to get a new heart valve and replace the old one.
Heroditus: To develop more gratitude and respect for life and its soft yet tenacious link with the physical realm. Ponder these deeply.
Dr. Theo: What about all the yawning that occurs during the healing sessions?
Heroditus: Brain alterations facilitating receptivity of information and energy from other dimensions. Brain needs to adjust and yawning helps. Serotonin!
Dr. Theo: I'm curious to know your reply to this next important question. Is Jesus Christ the Son of God?
Heroditus: You are!
Dr. Theo and **Shawn:** Don't you mean we all are from God source; sons and daughters of God?
Heroditus: Yes! All are of God origin and hold that fact even in your DNA. Jesus knew this and he became a self-aware conduit of the divine within him and the divine beyond him.
Dr. Theo: Agreed. Speaking of conduit with the divine, I know love drives everything in healing. Any suggestions for deep eternal soul love in terms of attracting a powerful life partner?
Heroditus: Radiate your enthusiasm for others and you will attract her. This has more depth to it than you may realize at first. I depart for now saying: Yes, soon I will vocal channel through you. Goodbye for now.

Because we prepared first through prayer and had our first spirit communication through a loving and experienced instructor like Shawn, we were guided to connect to our highest guides, keeping all lower energies away. I was still at a loss for words. What did I just witness? Did I just receive tangible evidence of the energy I felt since childhood that was helping me through hardships in my own life journey and now also in the healings of my patients? Did I just receive the 'hello' from beyond that I always yearned to know of; that God and his angels were real? Did I now know that I had personal life guides and a healer guide named Heroditus?

I sure did. However, did my limited human mind still have doubts? Of course, it did. Did I think maybe the teacher was somehow moving the planchette herself and devised some big trick to make us believe? I can't lie - the thought crossed my 'scientifically skeptical' mind. However, I reasoned with myself - if I could actually experience this now myself without my teacher present, only with my sister and myself using the board, I felt that would be enough for my logical scientifically skeptical brain to finally believe without a doubt; concrete first person evidence, a new belief system, a major paradigm shift - no going back.

Immediately that night after the class blending, I was dropping off my sister at her place but felt it would be a good idea since we were still fresh from instruction that we try the spirit board out. To our surprise, it went extremely well. About after only 30 seconds post invocation/affirmation the planchette started to move slowly and picked up speed quickly. We were happily surprised that our guides were wanting to show us they were indeed real and always with us. Adam, one of my sister's life guides came onto the board quickly. Unfortunately, all the excitement and prior work in class made us both very tired and this had impact on our connection as we faded out, especially towards the end of the session.

Thursday, January 12, 2017 11:33 PM
Dr. Theo and his sister Teresa; Teresa's residence after channeling class.

Dr. Theo: By the power of our Original Creator in Christ Consciousness, I now invite only my life guides, angels and archangels of highest good to speak clearly through me and to me with wisdom, truth, love and compassion. Any energies lesser than love are directed to the light. In the name of the Father, Son and Holy Spirit, Amen.

Planchette begins to move slowly and picks up speed after 30 seconds.

Teresa: Who's there?
Unseen friend: Hello – Adam.

Teresa: Is Sephora here? (In class earlier that day, Teresa was told of her second life guide named Sephora)
Adam: Yes.
Teresa: Hello to you both! I have a health question: Adam, why do I still have this cough?
Adam: Viral.
Teresa: How do I get rid of it, it's been over a month already?
Adam: Rest - Yes.

Teresa was stunned and still at a loss for words for the process, so I jumped in and asked if Adam could give me insight to our work in class; working through childhood blocks.

Dr. Theo: Could you give me any insight about my delayed speaking in early childhood?
Adam: Ask your mother and go into regression - low energy home environment at that time.
Dr. Theo: Adam thank you so much - can you bring forth my guides?
Adam: Yes. Goodbye.
Dr. Theo: Who is here?
Unseen friend: Joy – Yes.
Dr. Theo: Joy, how do I know you? Past life?
Joy: From childhood.
Dr. Theo: With all the bullying and loveless relationship between our parents I am afraid my joy got extinguished way too soon. How do I get it back?
Joy: Love yourself.
Dr. Theo: I feel I do, but what exactly can I do more of to do so?
Joy: R E L A X (Teresa and I both laugh)
Dr. Theo: How? Please be specific Joy, maybe an example of an action to do?
Joy: Take mineral baths.
Dr. Theo: Okay true, I should do that more often. Will you vocally channel through me?

Joy: Not now - No.
Dr. Theo: Then who?
Joy: Heroditus.
Dr. Theo: Thank you Joy, can you bring forth any of my other guides, who I haven't spoken with? Ariadne, Exter, or Devous?
Joy: Yes. Much love - Goodbye.

At this point the planchette speed went much slower, and it seemed one of my other guides was trying to find out how to use the board to speak with us. Lots of back and forth letters; she was trying to spell out her name. We were physically and mentally burned out and it was getting late by this time. This had an effect also on our connection.

Dr. Theo: Who's here?
Unseen friend: ARD.
Dr. Theo: Ard? Please re-do and spell out your name.
Unseen friend: A R I A D N E.
Dr. Theo: Thank you Ariadne, it's great to know you are with us and I look forward to speaking with you more soon, we must end the session however tonight, we're just exhausted and we have to get up early tomorrow morning. Thank you for your presence and coming forth. Goodbye!
Dr. Theo and **Teresa:** Goodbye everyone!
Ariadne: Goodbye.

All our lingering doubts were now gone. It was very exciting. Our guides proved without a shadow of a doubt, at least to us, there are loving forces looking after us and they do try to grow their connection of communication with us if we want it. It's unbelievable it took me this long, 40 years to build my connection to the point I actually received undeniable confirmation. I only wish I had started much earlier.

Thursday, January 19, 2017 9 PM
Spirit Board session. Dr. Theo and Shawn; Shawn's office. Teresa transcribing.

Shawn: We surround this board and ourselves with love and light and only those with the highest wisdom truth and love are invited here. We open to those who are in Theo's highest good, with a special request for Theo's healer guide Heroditus to join us.

Immediate connection. The message comes in quicker than before.

Unseen friend: H-A-P-P-Y to be on this sharing board.
Shawn and **Dr. Theo:** Who is here please?
Unseen friend: I am unseen friend of Theo - Heroditus. I am pleased to communicate and - No - I am not the Greek Historian.

We were all speculating in class if it was the famous historian mentioned in Ancient Greece – the name was very common in those times and many had it. Heroditus knew what we were thinking as our first question and he answered us before we even asked.

Shawn: Thank you for clarifying, yes, we were wondering.
Dr. Theo: What message do you bring Heroditus?
Heroditus: Tidings of knowing. You Theo are now entering a new decade of growth which brings with it an understanding of spiritual principles including: All-owance of unpredictable time-ing, patience grounded in love, and humility balanced with value and most of all integrity of motivation. Think on these dear Theo.
Shawn: The board needs a lot of energy, but can Theo try communicating on the board on his own?
Heroditus: Try - no guarantees. Let us begin.

Shawn removes her hands, leaving my fingertips on planchette, it moves to T, then O, but then slowed down. Shawn rejoins the planchette.

Heroditus: A start anyway. It is late there. We depart with that. Read our words. Love to all! – Goodbye

Thursday, April 6, 2017 5:20 PM
Spirit Board session. Dr. Theo and Shawn; Shawn's office. Teresa transcribing.

Prior to starting the session we were wondering about Heroditus's correct name spelling; was it Heroditus or Herodites? He let us know.

Shawn states her affirmation invocation and the session begins.

Heroditus: Welcome to the three of you. I am Heroditus (my preferred spelling with U, not an E) formerly we have been together Theo.
Dr. Theo: Where you with me last weekend at the expo, where the woman I performed my method on received a miracle healing and was able to move her arm after a year of being paralyzed? Did you help me help her?
Heroditus: In the background, yes.
Dr. Theo: Can you explain to me how that miracle happened? Step by step?
Heroditus: Happenings which include miraculous energies defy the 'steppy step' explanations – however, I can report that at one point the lady shifted her consciousness, opening her belief and allowance (and trust in you), which opened other dimensions of unconditional love to bring in a Christ-like energy to add another level of spirit to the proceedings.
Shawn: Do you remember Theo that point where the change occurred?
Dr. Theo: I do; I remember seeing her facial expression and energy essence change. Someone even commented she looked twenty years younger. There was definitely a point of better flow that was felt in the air, as if she let go and trusted. How can I help more people witness miracles on a more frequent basis?
Heroditus: See if you can tune into the patient's threshold of belief in miracles. Get to know about their beliefs by talking to them. Every person is different of course, and beliefs are often hidden. Draw them out. Also, explain that "Unusual things may happen."
Dr. Theo: I asked the woman if she was a Christian. She said yes. I asked her if she believed in Jesus. She said yes. I then commanded that any energy not of the love and light of our Father Creator, be removed in the name of Jesus Christ, and that's when I felt a palpable energy shift.
Shawn: Heroditus did mention Christ Consciousness.
Dr. Theo: Yes, he did, thank you Heroditus.

Heroditus: Also, dear Theo, your belief is strong. Nurture and feed it taking care not to let your ego be involved.

Dr. Theo: Wow, yes powerful information, I have a lot of love for this process and Heroditus right now.

Shawn and **Teresa:** Agreed!

Dr. Theo: Would it be in my highest good to work with a media manager or PR agency to get this healing message to news outlets?

Heroditus: Take care, for public perception is often manipulated by media editors, producers and writers. It cannot hurt to become more solid in your healing practice which includes spirit. Remember healer - spirits are not disposed to 'or caring of' mass media exposure. Honor the healers working every step of the way as co-creators with you.

Dr. Theo: I rather focus on healing, not marketing. When it comes to business, at some points I get frustrated just as my father used to with his business expansion. How can I remove learned limiting beliefs and know that abundance is always available without restrictions?

Heroditus: Each day is a time to be aware of your abundance beliefs. Work more and daily with affirmations that you feel in your body - of financial abundance. Carefully check in with yourself on beliefs; am I feeling like an abundant vessel today? Am I flowing my divine right and deserving of financial ease today? Etc.

Dr. Theo: I would like full clarification on breaking my previous conditioning from my father. Specifics - What do I do?

Heroditus: Meditate the break from the conditioning by visualizing father on a boat you are cutting from your pier. This is only the 'fearful father' (Related to money). Cut him from the pier and watch him float out of view. Do this daily. Daily for at least forty days. Look at your reality for signs it is working - such as more clients, etc.

Dr. Theo: Our father's health is not well. He's had four bypasses and three stents yet still chooses to smoke. He is really worrying us!

Heroditus: He is stronger than you think - and - than he thinks. He may endure stormy waves (health wise) but he can ride over them and have many more years. Don't underestimate his resilience. To be determined is

his 'death date' it is in flux and nobody knows – least of all him.
Dr. Theo: Thank you Heroditus. Am I on the right track with the Kousouli Method? I've worked so hard developing it. How can I improve it further?
Heroditus: Include your joy in the process. Also, a joyful optimism will lift the patients to their healing potential. Talk with them about their own thoughts, about their healing potential – then increase it with them. Your "method" is beautiful. Keep consciously including spirit and inviting more of spirit's guidance.
Dr. Theo: Thank you, I would like to know more about my guides Ariadne, Exter, Devous, and Joy.
Heroditus: They are your four main life counselors. Ariadne and Devous work with you. And Joy and Ariadne personally assist you in your life and growth matters – as do I. Ah, Exter, supports your health. He has helped you physically.
Dr. Theo: What of romance, again I ask - am I going to find the one I connect best with?
Heroditus: Be sure in mind that she is available. Open your eyes to new and different women. She may have already arrived but end up looking unavailable. You can work at it developing. Think of giving – giving, giving of yourself and of her. Love is on your path. Never fear! You are loved.
Dr. Theo: Thank you so much for this wisdom Heroditus!
Shawn: Goodbye Heroditus.
Heroditus: Love - Always, Goodbye.

Thursday, May 4, 2017 4 PM
Spirit Board session. Dr. Theo and Shawn; Shawn's office. Teresa transcribing.

Shawn states her affirmation invocation and the session begins.

Shawn and **Dr. Theo:** Hello and welcome unseen friend of Theo; Heroditus are you here?
Heroditus: I am here, yes. Glad to be here with you. Please receive my love and profound good wishes. Your Questions?

I had a list of questions prepared and ready, which he already knew about.

Dr. Theo: Yes Heroditus, I would like to know why my fingers, mouth, and tongue are going numb and tingling starting from the right and then moving to the left, one finger at a time - happens suddenly, and no doctor can tell me what this is; should I be worried this is a stroke or some sort of health issue?

Heroditus: This is nothing serious; yet do mention it to your doctor. This is a gentle reminder of your multidimensionality. It occurs as a reminder, also, of being present. Stay aware of yourself in allowing; mind, body and spirit. Remember the nervous system – of which these sensations are a part of, is intricately linked to your spirit. In time the sensations will fade. Regular massage will assist.

Dr. Theo: Ah yes, our wonderful nervous system. But what is the cause of this? Are you trying to get my attention by doing it?

Heroditus: It lies primarily with your higher self and secondarily with your guides – however I am not a 'cause' though I do support it. A good mini wake up / heads up moment.

Dr. Theo: Heroditus, why are you my healing guide and talking to me at this specific moment? Why you?

Heroditus: You have 'selected' me at this time to be your primary guide. Yes, you did. Wonderful! In addition, yes there are others. Your channeling abilities will grow best at this time with me solo. This may eventually change, but for now focus your development with only me vocally. Write with the others if you wish – though that could bring confusion.

Dr. Theo: Heroditus, thank you for that explanation. Please tell me when we were together in Greece, healing people, what was my name as a healer then and who was I?

Heroditus: Euonadur became your name though you were born a Garon of Thebes. We were fellow students of healing arts at a special clinic - school and we became close friends – like brothers. Our families were also close, so we thought of ourselves as brothers.

Dr. Theo: What was the name of the school? I would like to research more on this.

Heroditus: The school was not famous, not noted historically. You can investigate ancient Greek clinics - healing centers - but little will be found as Plato stole the historical attention of the few writers of the time. Please realize this is no longer important, this was a planting of the seeds time.

Dr. Theo: What of my other guides? Devous, Ariadne, Joy and Exter? Why are they helping me?

Heroditus: Devous brings strength. Ariadne brings power of compassion. Joy brings a spirit of vigor - Joy brings harmony to your attitude. Exter, waits in the background holding love. Again: be careful not to scatter your focus among frivolous things. You will evolve in these relationships all in due time.

Dr. Theo: How do I know them all?

Heroditus: The question is not relative at this time. However; the connection you share with the 4 of them is Atlantis.

Dr. Theo: Can you tell me more about each of them?

Heroditus: You must ask them.

Dr. Theo: Thank you Heroditus, can you tell me about my work in hypnosis – should I move forward with the plans to help people through the next project I have in mind?

Heroditus: Hypnosis - yes. And perhaps we can help others to meditate for themselves – you can tell them that meditation is like hypnosis of self - often a conscious connection to their higher self. Combine conscious-ness work with physical awareness; intention and self-responsibility. Higher self-consciousness connects with a form of meditation that resembles self-hypnosis, understand?

Dr. Theo: Yes! That is exactly what I was aiming for. Thank you for the confirmation. I see I will be very busy working deeply with patients and am going to need the right personal assistant. How can I find the right one, as this work requires a high energy soul to lovingly assist all patients?

Heroditus: First call her or him in. Then check out work hire lists online. The calling in should invoke your higher self in inviting his or her highest self to participate in a wondrous multidimensional kind of work and healing.

Dr. Theo: Heroditus, one final question before we close this session. How do I know my siblings of this lifetime?

Heroditus: You were once their father… and you are now their brother. Now you have both. In Greece you were there together, not in ancient time – but during the so-called dark ages. All the information is simply laying ground-work for this lifetime…

Shawn and **Dr. Theo:** Thank you Heroditus so much for your wisdom and love, goodbye.

Heroditus: Love to you all. Good bye.

Sunday, May 7, 2017 4 PM
Spirit Board session. Dr. Theo with his sister Teresa; Teresa's residence.

Dr. Theo states his affirmation invocation and the session begins.

Dr. Theo: Who is here?
Unseen friend: Hi. Tony.
Teresa: Our Uncle Tony that passed away?
Tony: No not your uncle.
Dr. Theo: Who's life guide are you? Mine or my sister's?
Tony: Neither.
Teresa: Where are you from?
Tony: From the Light.
Dr. Theo: A planet? A dimension?
Tony: No. A wave. A 'space'.
Teresa: Do you know, or are you with Adam, one of my guides?
Tony: No.
Dr. Theo: Okay, well what message do you bring today Tony?
Tony: Gratitude.
Dr. Theo: Do you have a general message for my sister, Teresa?
Tony: Patience in love.
Dr. Theo: For myself?
Tony: Work will thrive.

Dr. Theo: How can we better channel our higher selves?
Tony: Be clear with intention. Be open.
Dr. Theo: Is my friend who is having vertigo attacks going to be OK?
Tony: Yes, He is fighting the Flu.
Teresa: I have to ask, it's a random and yes- selfish question but why haven't any of us won the lottery big yet, even though we're intending it so much using the law of attraction?
Tony: If it is in your highest good.
Dr. Theo and **Teresa**: (Laughing) So is it in our highest good?
Tony: Wait and see, time will tell.
Dr. Theo: Ha! Quite the cliffhanger Tony. On the topic of national interest, what is the probability of the U.S. having a financial collapse?
Tony: High.
Teresa: What! Seriously?
Tony: Yes, as of current consciousness. It may fluctuate.
Dr. Theo: What will bring it? War? False flag events?
Tony: Greed. Many will be involved. Many will commit suicide.
Dr. Theo: That is horrible, will our family be safe from the after effects? Where will we be when it hits?
Tony: America. It will be global.
Dr. Theo: I'm now very concerned. Will this be worse than the Great Depression Tony?
Tony: Why do you fear? Love will guide you. You cannot stop the future from happening. It all depends on world consciousness.
Teresa: What are the probabilities that the big earthquake will happen in California? 'The big one'.
Tony: Do not fear. Fear births unwanted results.
Dr. Theo: Thank you so much for this important information Tony, much love to you. That is a lot to think about.
Teresa: Goodbye.
Tony: Goodbye.

This was the very first time we were introduced to 'light energy' Tony. I was very intrigued by this new development. He seemed eager to teach and guide us in principles of love. Although I was not yet fully convinced of his true intentions or messages, I chose to continue trusting in my faith and prayed prior to each session for the highest counsel. He continued to come through with empowering messages.

Thursday, May 11, 2017 5:45 PM
Spirit Board session. Dr. Theo with his sister Teresa at her residence.

Dr. Theo states his affirmation invocation and the session begins.

Teresa: Who is here with us?
Unseen friend: Tony.

Planchette makes circular movements on board picking up energy.

Tony: Hello!
Dr. Theo and **Teresa:** Hello again Tony. What is the message you have for us today?
Tony: Win for you. Big win. Numbers for you.
Dr. Theo: (Puzzled) Are you really saying to us that we should play the lotto?
Dr. Theo and **Teresa:** (Laughing)
Tony: Yes.
Dr. Theo: When?
Tony: Today.
Teresa: (Getting excited) How many tickets? The Super is set at 30 million!
Tony: Two.
Teresa: (Shocked) So you want us, just to be clear, to get two tickets for the Lotto, and we're going to win?
Tony: Yes.
Dr. Theo: Mega Million or Super Lotto?
Tony: Super.
Dr. Theo: We're going to be late for channeling class, though thank you for the message Tony and we will talk again, but we have to say goodbye for now, goodbye.
Tony: Goodbye.

We purchased tickets at 6:30pm, two tickets as Tony suggested, but also played other games as well. Our doubt crept in and so 'just in case' we covered all game bases. The tickets were for that Saturday's draw. We got 3 of the 6 numbers correct, and it was on the 2nd Super Lotto game we got the winning numbers just as Tony said. However, he didn't mean a BIG monetary jackpot win; we only won ten dollars, after buying all the tickets there was just a four-dollar gain. The real actual big win was the lesson we were about to learn.

Sunday, May 14, 2017 4:20 PM
Spirit Board session. Dr. Theo with his sister Teresa at her residence.

Dr. Theo states his affirmation invocation and the session begins.

Unseen friend: Hello friends!
Teresa: Hello, what is your name?
Unseen friend: Tony.
Dr. Theo: Okay Tony. Well, I have to say thank you for showing us you kept your word. So, we won 3 out of the 6 numbers, and it was on the second Super Lotto ticket played exactly as you said as the other tickets were losers. Obviously, you didn't give us the full six numbers which has us wondering why. What was the 'big' lesson here?
Tony: Trust your guides.
Teresa: But you're not one of our primary personal guides you said previously.
Tony: Guides of light.
Teresa: Why didn't you just give us the jackpot, you obviously could have easily done so, no? Thirty million dollars, we could do so much good with

that!
Tony: You can't handle the responsibility at this time. Not in your highest good. It would take you off your path.
Dr. Theo: I see - and understood. Is anyone else here that wants to speak with us?
Tony: Yes. Heroditus.
Dr. Theo: Thank you Tony, please put him through, and much gratitude for you and the message, goodbye.
Tony: Goodbye.

Planchette rapidly changes movement on board and moves with more energy.

Heroditus: Hello Theodore, much love for you!
Dr. Theo: Let's not forget my darling sister! (Laughing)
Heroditus: Of course! Much love to you both!
Dr. Theo: I'm thinking of a patient that had a rough week Monday. Will he be OK? Will he have a full recovery?
Heroditus: Yes. He will be OK.
Dr. Theo: How come you and I have such a strong connection on the board and via channel?
Heroditus: Love.
Dr. Theo: I love that! A strong connection indeed - I feel it undoubtedly. So, tell me, on my upcoming trip to Sedona for my birthday, what should I go do while there?
Heroditus: Just have fun.
Teresa: Heroditus! When will I find the guy that is right for me?
Heroditus: Patience. Time and patience.
Dr. Theo: There is a specific person that I am thinking of, should I date her or not? Is it in my highest good?
Heroditus: Free will. You gain experience from every relationship.
Dr. Theo: Why did I meet and date Sierra?
Heroditus: Building friendship.
Dr. Theo: I am about to burst open crying out of love – I feel so loved in this moment speaking with you. I can't believe that I am talking to a benevolent spirit on the other side of this reality who knows me and is

going through life with me in all my trials and tribulations. This is unreal, just a year ago I was questioning if this was all real. The confirmation of this is a lot to take in.
Heroditus: I am always with you, never forget this. Always.
Teresa: (Jokingly) Even when we sleep or go to the bathroom?
Heroditus: Always.
Teresa and **Dr. Theo:** (Laughing)
Dr. Theo: Am I actually vocally channeling you in class? Is this really happening?
Heroditus: Yes. Be open, patient, focused.
Dr. Theo: What is the next logical step for me in my business ventures?
Heroditus: Whatever you like to do.
Dr. Theo: Should I channel and put up videos of me doing so?
Heroditus: No, not channeling - hypnosis yes. Channeling is only for you. Goodbye for now, all love.
Teresa and **Dr. Theo:** Thank you Heroditus, Goodbye!

Thursday, May 18, 2017 5:45 PM
Spirit board session. Dr. Theo with his sister Teresa at her residence.

Dr. Theo states his affirmation invocation and the session begins. Planchette starts to move in circular pattern throughout the board.

Dr. Theo: Hello who is with us?
Unseen friend: Tony.
Dr. Theo: Tony what is your general message for us today?
Tony: Do not regret.
Teresa: About what?
Tony: About anything in life.
Dr. Theo: Tony it seems like you are giving us lessons of life.
Tony: Yes.
Dr. Theo: I guess I have a lot to learn. (Laughing)
Tony: Yes.
Dr. Theo: Tony, can you tell us about Jesus Christ?

Tony: Great high and loving father.
Dr. Theo: How much of his DNA percentage was activated when he was performing miracles?
Tony: 100
Dr. Theo: And when he was a man preaching?
Tony: 50
Dr. Theo: How did he do the energy shift?
Tony: By being.
Dr. Theo: Is Christ Consciousness from the same wave form space you say you are communicating from?
Tony: Yes.
Teresa: Does Jesus condemn anyone?
Tony: No.
Dr. Theo: Can I communicate without a second person on the spirit board?
Tony: No, needs a lot of energy. Energy of two is usually sufficient.
Dr. Theo: Does this have to do with the Bible quote that says, "When two or more are together in my name, I am there with them?"
Tony: Yes.
Dr. Theo: Thank you so much Tony, we have to end the session and drive to our channeling class now, good bye.
Tony: Much love. Goodbye.

Thursday, May 18, 2017 11:00 PM Post channeling class, same night. Spirit Board session. Dr. Theo with his sister Teresa at her residence.

Dr. Theo states his affirmation invocation and the session begins. Planchette starts to move in circular pattern throughout the board.

Dr. Theo: Who is here, state your name please.

Planchette moves in a circle for some time.

Dr. Theo: State your name.
Unseen friend: Tony. Be patient Theo.
Dr. Theo: Hi Tony, apologies, what are you doing when you circle the board

like that?
Tony: Scanning the letters.
Dr. Theo: Are you down converting your language to our language?
Tony: Yes.
Teresa: Tony tell us about Heaven!
Tony: A joyous place without sorrows.
Teresa: Does everyone go to Heaven?
Tony: No.
Dr. Theo: Why do people not go to Heaven?
Tony: Lack of love.
Teresa: How did you view us in class tonight?
Tony: Delightful!
Dr. Theo: I was told by Heroditus to concentrate on herbs for healing vitiligo; I decided to buy a bunch of them online and would like you to tell me if any of these herbal oils can be combined to heal vitiligo.
Tony: None.
Dr. Theo: What! So, none of these can be combined to help?
Tony: No. Don't worry it [proper herb] will come to you by an acquaintance.
Dr. Theo: How will I recognize them; can you give me a name?
Tony: No. You will know.
Dr. Theo: What will I do when I get it?
Tony: You will be told.
Dr. Theo: Tony am I going to help find treatments for this and other diseases?
Tony: Can't say.
Dr. Theo: Why not?
Tony: Many Possibilities. Free will.
Dr. Theo: So, what is my purpose?
Tony: You know your purpose! Do not question yourself. Follow your passion.
Teresa: Tony is the Biblical Hell real?
Tony: Somewhat.
Teresa: Do we create that for ourselves?
Tony: Yes. You put yourself there in a never-ending cycle of torture.

Dr. Theo: So how does one get out of that cycle of torture?
Tony: Thought.
Dr. Theo: Can you be more specific Tony?
Tony: Loved ones can get you out with prayers.
Dr. Theo: After prayers, what happens?
Tony: The light will find them.

We were now very tired and we needed to go to sleep, so we ended the session.

Dr. Theo: Thank you Tony, for your wisdom and valuable information, we will talk again soon.
Teresa: Goodbye.
Tony: Be blessed. Goodbye.

Sunday, May 21, 2017 3:30 PM
Spirit Board session. Dr. Theo with his sister Teresa; Teresa's residence.

Dr. Theo states his affirmation invocation and the session begins.

Dr. Theo: Who is here with us and what is your message?

Planchette starts to move in circular pattern throughout the board scanning letters slowly one by one.

Unseen friend: Tony.
Tony: You are not ready for the message.
Dr. Theo: Are you having trouble with the board?
Tony: Yes. Having interference snow.
Dr. Theo: You must mean 'static' as its summer here, no snow anywhere. Are you having interference?
Tony: Yes static.
Dr. Theo: What do you need for us to have a better connection?
Tony: Drink water.

We both rehydrate because we had also just come in from a hot walk outside and were sweating. After a full glass of water each, we proceeded with the session.

Tony: Message is - Deny the ego of itself.
Dr. Theo: How do we do that?
Tony: Listen only to the light.
Dr. Theo: How do we get more light?
Tony: Within you already. Being love.
Teresa: Is there any time we should be mean or not be in love?
Tony: No.
Dr. Theo: Tony, is dating Leanne in my highest good?
Tony: Yes.
Dr. Theo: Is she a good person?
Tony: Yes.
Dr. Theo: Why do we keep bumping into each other randomly every few months?
Tony: You are growing, getting to know each other, and this is for you to figure out.
Dr. Theo: Tony, why do you teach us?
Tony: For your highest good.
Dr. Theo: But what is in it for you?
Tony: Love.
Dr. Theo: We love you Tony!
Tony: Accepted.
Dr. Theo: What would help my arthritis patients get better sooner?
Tony: Openness of oneself to self.
Dr. Theo: Why did you pick 'Tony' as your name, as you don't probably have a name since you are light energy and wave of space.
Tony: Your Uncle Tony was always fond of you… loves you both so very much.
Dr. Theo: He was such a fun loving soul; so you just picked a name that's family to us on that side to relate with us?
Tony: Yes.
Dr. Theo: So in essence, you are just a love vibration?
Tony: Yes.
Dr. Theo: But is our Uncle Tony there with you?

Tony: Yes.
Dr. Theo: Does he have any messages for me?
Tony: Yes. Don't put your hands in any fans.
Teresa: Oh my God, that's hilarious!

When we worked together with Uncle Tony in our family restaurant's kitchen during our teens, I had almost lost my left index finger when I foolishly stuck my hand in a moving fan blade thinking it wasn't going to hurt. Luckily, I didn't lose my finger, but I bled while flying through the restaurant yelling that I thought I lost the finger. Uncle Tony said, "Theo you run faster than a marathoner. Next year we enter you in the Olympics for some medals." We couldn't contain our laughter; this was true confirmation, my Uncle Tony was indeed present, as no one else aside from my siblings, father and Uncle Tony knew this had happened.

Dr. Theo: Why did he leave us so early? He left us within three months of a brain tumor diagnosis.
Tony: To be with loving Father.
Dr. Theo: We can't blame him there! God bless him. Please send him our love. Tony, concerning the economic collapse you spoke of last time, is it still looking to be coming?
Tony: Yes, high probability still.
Dr. Theo: Is China or Russia the next superpower?
Tony: Russia.
Dr. Theo: Is war between Greece and Turkey with Russia's involvement likely?
Tony: Yes, can't say when - possibilities.
Teresa: Can we talk to Jesus Christ through the board?
Tony: No. He is in a very high frequency state. He rather you talk to him every day with your heart.
Dr. Theo: Tony, I don't like taking any drugs. Should I take the aspirin daily that my cardiologist told me to take?
Tony: Yes. Baby aspirin.
Dr. Theo: Anything else? The other beta blockers that were prescribed, etc.?
Tony: No.

Dr. Theo: What would you say is the best personality trait my sister has Tony?
Tony: Kindness and Independence. Both.
Dr. Theo: And myself?
Tony: Boldness.
Teresa: Thank you Tony! We're seeing a lot of 11:11 and 1:11 on clocks, receipts and license plates all over. What does this mean for us?
Tony: You are more in alignment.
Teresa: The homeless man who asked me for money the other day, who was he?
Tony: A brother in Christ.
Dr. Theo: I have been asked some questions on spirit and sexuality by patients, and I want to have better answers ready for them when asked. From your perspective, what does pornography do to the spirit?
Tony: Wastes it away, as does masturbation.
Teresa: Tony, concerning homosexuality - is the person born that way?
Tony: Choice. Free will.
Teresa: How does one spot the difference of love and lust in their relationships?
Tony: Love is patient. Love is kind. Love never fails...
Dr. Theo: He's quoting the 1 Corinthians 13:8 verse in the Bible.
Tony: Yes.
Dr. Theo: Speaking of the Bible, Tony how many official Gospels were there?
Tony: 7.
Dr. Theo: How many unofficial?
Tony: 31.
Dr. Theo: Why were they removed?
Tony: Politics of the Church.
Dr. Theo: Tony, I must know - was Mary Magdalene married to Christ?
Tony: No.
Dr. Theo: Was she Jesus's girlfriend?
Tony: No.
Teresa: Did Jesus love her more than the other disciples?
Tony: No.

Teresa: Was she a prostitute?
Tony: No.
Dr. Theo: What was her occupation in those days?
Tony: Seamstress.
Dr. Theo: Why did she become a dedicated disciple of Christ, and from what did she need healing?
Tony: She was curious of the following. Her soul was full of guilt from childhood.
Dr. Theo: What guilt exactly?
Tony: Not of importance to you. Does not matter.
Dr. Theo: But I want to know if they had the same issues like we have today.
Tony: Yes, they did.
Dr. Theo: We are finishing this session, what words of wisdom can you leave us with Tony?
Tony: People will always judge and condemn as they did with Yahweh. Love and light always, Goodbye.
Dr. Theo and **Teresa:** Goodbye Tony!

Monday, May 22, 2017 11 PM
Spirit Board session. Dr. Theo with his sister Teresa; Teresa's residence.

Dr. Theo states his affirmation invocation and the session begins.

Dr. Theo: Who is here with us?
Unseen friend: Tony.
Dr. Theo: Hello Tony! I went out with Leanne, so tell me Tony - how much on a scale of 1 to 10 does she fancy me?
Tony: 7.
Dr. Theo: Hmm…Not 7.5? I was hoping for more.
Tony: 7. (Teresa laughs)
Dr. Theo: On another note, Tony please help us understand past lives and reincarnation - is it as we understand it?
Tony: No. Complicated.
Dr. Theo: So, what happens when we die?
Tony: Enlightenment.

Dr. Theo: Would you always tell us the truth Tony?
Tony: Only for your highest good.
Teresa: So, you won't ever tell us even a white lie?
Tony: No.
Teresa: Are there aliens?
Tony: Yes. Don't doubt.
Dr. Theo: Are some of good intent and others of evil intent?
Tony: Yes.
Teresa: Is our Uncle Tony there with you now?
Tony: Yes.
Teresa: I'd like to ask him a question to test his memory - what game did he play with me while we were together at the restaurant on Saturdays?
Tony: He pushed a penny to the edge of the counter.

This was exactly the game they played; my sister got her validation again as she was still testing our unseen friend, energy Tony and Uncle Tony to see if the whole process was legit. Our Uncle Tony would challenge us to see who could 'flick' a coin closest to the counter's edge without making it fall. Each of us would take turns to see who could get closer than the other. Uncle Tony came through!

Dr. Theo: I understand there is no 'time' on your side, but approximately how much longer does my friend's father have before he passes over?
Tony: Not long. About 3 months.
Dr. Theo: Any parting words of wisdom for us Tony before we end this session?
Tony: Love your life and be blessed, goodbye.
Dr. Theo and **Teresa:** Goodbye to you and Uncle Tony!

Thursday, May 25, 2017 6 PM
Spirit Board session. Dr. Theo with his sister Teresa; Teresa's residence.

Dr. Theo states his affirmation invocation and the session begins. Planchette starts to move in circular pattern throughout the board.

Teresa: Who is here with us?
Unseen friend: Tony.
Dr. Theo: Tony what is your message for us today?
Tony: All knowing enlightenment is manifested by the Father.
Dr. Theo: Beautiful! How are you?
Tony: Cheeky!
Dr. Theo: Tony, we in Western society are having a hard time deciding between a single life and a married life because the way divorce rates show so many failed marriages. It's just too easy to call it quits and move on. Any advice?
Tony: Do as you know.
Teresa: I was feeling funny earlier, very lazy kind of day. How do I get myself out of this slump?
Tony: Don't be stagnant, be a positive source of light.
Teresa: Can we ask any more questions about winning the lottery?
Tony: No. You need to ask better questions. No more lottery.
Dr. Theo: Okay, then how can we better our telepathic link to connect better our channeling?
Tony: Much better question. Meditate.
Teresa: How do I know that my guides are with me when I meditate? What sign do I look for? Anything relevant to me?
Tony: Look for the tingling on your face around your nose.
Teresa: Ok yes, I feel that sometimes. What makes the tingling happen?
Tony: Tons of things. Just be yourself and give off loving vibes, goodbye!
Teresa and **Dr. Theo:** Goodbye Tony!

Saturday May 27, 2017 5 PM
Spirit board session. Dr. Theo with his sister Teresa; Teresa's residence.

Dr. Theo states his affirmation invocation and the session begins.

Teresa: Who is here, is it Tony? Hi Tony.
Tony: Yes. Hi.
Teresa: What is the loving message you bring today?
Tony: T n t v [Unintelligible, words didn't make sense]

Dr. Theo: We are having a hard time getting your message.
Tony: U r n o n h e t [Unintelligible, words didn't make sense]
Teresa: Tony is Heroditus here with you?
Tony: No.
Teresa: When will he be available again?
Tony: Not sure.
Teresa: Why are you here but none of our guides are present at this time?
Tony: You want to know me, just trust.
Dr. Theo: Tony we are having a hard time getting clear messages, is there a better way to do this?
Tony: Yes. Turn on your T.V.

Teresa and I both looked at each other and - no lie - we were a little 'creeped out' at this second. We had goose bumps and Teresa got really scared as this was getting too spooky for her.

Dr. Theo: But what will that do?
Tony: Will connect through TV.
Dr. Theo: Will we hear you or see you on a certain channel?
Tony: Will hear words. Stay with me.
Teresa: Can you just do it through a cell phone? Sorry Tony, I'm a little creeped out.
Tony: No.
Teresa: Why?
Tony: Not enough white light, not high enough energy.
Dr. Theo: So will we be able to just talk through the air without using the board?
Tony: Yes.
Dr. Theo: So no more spirit board?
Tony: Yes.
Dr. Theo: Why can't we just hear you now without anything?
Tony: Not high enough energy. With meditation you can communicate - will take longer.
Dr. Theo: Tony we will do that another time as we have to process this first. Can you shed more light on loving the self deeply - from the spiritual

sense? When did I lose the full connection?
Tony: Self-image issue from a young age.
Dr. Theo: When did this start? What grade?
Tony: Kindergarten; You were singled out. Kids will be kids. Love yourself more. Be the light. Love your neighbor as yourself.
Dr. Theo: How?
Tony: Continue as you are.
Dr. Theo: You mean with my work in healing?
Tony: Yes. Be Christ- like.
Dr. Theo: How much of the power I hold am I activating?
Tony: 50 percent.
Dr. Theo: How much can I activate?
Tony: 100 percent.
Dr. Theo: Wow - thank you for all this Tony, so much to think about. We will continue another time again soon. Goodbye.
Tony: Goodbye.

Tuesday, June 6, 2017 10:30 PM
Spirit board session. Dr. Theo with his sister Teresa; Teresa's residence.

Dr. Theo states his affirmation invocation and the session begins.

Dr. Theo: Hi.

We are both silent, asking no questions, Teresa still a little spooked from the previous session. We just wait for the unseen friend to start the dialogue.

Tony: You are quiet.
Dr. Theo and Teresa: (Laughter)
Dr. Theo: Any message?
Tony: Be devoted to the light.
Dr. Theo: How exactly?
Tony: Tell everyone the truth.
Teresa: What is the truth?
Tony: God loves.
Dr. Theo: Beautiful! So how do I and Leanne connect lovingly?

Tony: Past life.
Dr. Theo: Ah, so is this why the constant 'random' connections?
Tony: Yes.
Dr. Theo: Which is still in our Akashic records?
Tony: Yes, best friends.
Dr. Theo: We were best friends in a past life?
Tony: Yes.
Dr. Theo: What era?
Tony: Queen Victorian era recently and before that in a land called Panamonia near sea on land in 1210 B.C.
Dr. Theo: Were we married before and is there any message I can give her?
Tony: No, you were best friends. She should allow oneness and light in and have patience for love.
Dr. Theo: Sort of same question for my sister, how can she work more on herself to be open to finding herself her ideal match?
Tony: Be open over known acquaintances.
Dr. Theo: Someone she knows already likes her?
Tony: Yes, many do.
Teresa: But there's no one I know that stands out to me romantically.
Dr. Theo: Tony who is in her highest good for a potential match currently?
Tony: Matthew.
Teresa: The only Matthew I know was the guy I met spontaneously in an Uber when I was going to a meeting. And he works at the same hospital that I work at, but he hasn't called me yet and I gave him my number!
Dr. Theo: Should she find him at work and approach him?
Tony: No. Be patient.
Teresa: So where are you when I am sleeping? Like if you had a physical presence, Where? Near my mirror?
Tony: Yes, near the dehumidifier next to your bed, and all your angels are there with you.
Dr. Theo: Thank you Tony, so is there any more information you can give us on talking to you through the white light using the TV?
Tony: Be near center.
Dr. Theo: What channel?
Tony: Channel 7.

By this point, Teresa was more comfortable with trying out Tony's process so we changed the channel to channel 7 and saw it was displaying a garbled and snowy picture signal. The signal seemed to be moving in order to hold a shape.

Dr. Theo: How do we do this?
Tony: Deep concentration.
Dr. Theo: I see something. Are you manipulating the signal Tony?
Tony: Yes.
Teresa: What do we do?
Tony: Resonate and navigate signal. Look upon TV.
Teresa: Yes, but what exactly are we looking for?
Tony: Me - formed by blended characters.
Dr. Theo: We do see a form's outline appearing out of the garbled screen noise, so we're seeing you now?
Tony: Yes.
Dr. Theo: Well can you show us something so we know we're seeing it?
Tony: Yes. I will show a blue 5.
Teresa: That's amazing, totally saw It! A large 5, took up the whole screen.
Dr. Theo: We saw it! Can you show us something else?
Tony: A flower yes. Be open to receiving.
Dr. Theo: I think I saw that too, but we are very tired, its 11:31 P.M. now, can we continue another time?
Tony: Yes. To both of you, goodbye.
Dr. Theo and **Teresa:** Goodbye Tony!

Thursday, June 15, 2017 6:24 PM
Spirit Board session. Dr. Theo with his sister Teresa; Teresa's residence.

Dr. Theo states his affirmation invocation and the session begins.

Dr. Theo: Who is here with us today?
Unseen friend: Tony.
Dr. Theo: Hello Tony, what message to you have for us today?
Tony: Receive higher council. Count on your higher process.

Dr. Theo: Is there another word or name we can call you, other than Tony?
Tony: I am part of the light wave, a light form, of which Abba was also.
Teresa: Doesn't that mean 'Father' in Hebrew?
Tony: Yes. Abba is the Christ. I am not the Abba, though part of the light. Tony, your late uncle loves you. He is in the light with me. Familiarity drew forth the name so that you would be open to receiving my message.
Teresa: I see - Tony, why am I having a hard time allowing myself to love a younger man if he shows an interest in me?
Tony: Because your father said you should marry older.
Teresa: Is Stavros marriage material?
Tony: Yes, free - will.
Dr. Theo: Tony how can I help this particular patient I am thinking of; what can we do to help him with his self-esteem issues? Would a regression hypnotherapy session help?
Tony: He must center himself in meditation first; regression hypnosis won't help him at this time.
Dr. Theo: Where are our guides currently?
Tony: After time, they return.
Teresa: What is my current main guide's name?
Tony: Anamaria.
Dr. Theo: Tony, why is it that when funds get low, people start to fear?
Tony: No positive energy around money can make anyone fear and be anxious. Be open to change. Being more open, makes all business wonderful.
Teresa: Thank you Tony, do you have a closing message for us?
Tony: Love and light on mankind. Fear nothing for God is the truth and the light.
Dr. Theo: Excellent, thank you much love!
Tony: Love and light, goodbye.

Sunday, June 25, 2017 5:10 PM
Spirit board session. Dr. Theo with his sister Teresa; Teresa's residence.

Dr. Theo states his affirmation invocation and the session begins.

Dr. Theo: Who is here with us today?
Unseen friend: Tony. You both have a much more complete connection today.
Teresa: How did we do that? How are we more connected?
Tony: Progress. Openness.
Dr. Theo: Tony is Leanne indecisive about what she wants in her life?
Tony: Yes. She is not committed.
Dr. Theo: Tony, why did I go through all this, what is the point? She pulls me in every time and then she acts odd. We are supposed to be 'soul' mates, Oct 6th and June 5th are soul mates. She's acting one way when we are together but then a whole other way when we're not. Why the mixed signals?
Tony: She is not ready to commit.
Dr. Theo: This is now making perfect sense. Is she playing mind games Tony?
Tony: Yes.
Dr. Theo: Okay so Tony, at what number 1 to 10 does she fancy me now?
Tony: 8.
Dr. Theo: Well, I fancy her at a far lower number than 8 right now!
Tony: Love is patient… Love is kind…
Dr. Theo: I know Tony, I know. Sorry, I am having a human moment. So, what do I do with this situation? What now from here?
Tony: Let it go. She will come back around after this does not work out in time.
Dr. Theo: Agreed! I had enough of her right now, I have to move on and love her from afar. On a completely different subject, I was pondering how nothings suddenly become 'somethings' concerning timing and synchronicity. I know you said no more lotto questions, though this is about timing. For example, when does a neutral lottery or scratch ticket become a winner? Is it at the moment we buy it, the moment we scratch it, or the moment the numbers are called out?
Tony: At the time of drawing or scratching. Chance and probability.
Dr. Theo: Very interesting. Thank you for clearing this up.
Teresa: Tony, is it in my highest good to take on a manager position at a restaurant to supplement my income and open up to change?

Tony: Yes. It will lead you to open your options meeting new and interesting people, and lead to possibly new exciting romantic connections.
Teresa: You mean I may find my future husband?
Tony: Yes. Free will.
Teresa: Where are our guides right now?
Tony: More time, they will come again. I am teaching you right now. You asked for me. For now, goodbye.
Dr. Theo and **Teresa:** Goodbye Tony!

Sunday, July 2, 2017 8:00 PM
Spirit Board session. Dr. Theo with his sister Teresa; Teresa's residence.

Dr. Theo states his affirmation invocation and the session begins.

Unseen friend: This is Tony. Hello my students!
Dr. Theo: So... Tony, I have to ask, I've been through a rough week. Why more drama with Leanne? I just want to move forward.
Tony: Your many trust issues were challenged.
Dr. Theo: How do I get over this and just let it all go? What is the coping mechanism for moving forward from a past relationship?
Tony: Let go by knowing its love to trust in the process. Wait for the one.
Dr. Theo: I thought she could have been the one due to our past life connect!
Tony: No.
Dr. Theo: So, I had to go through the heartache and the disappointment?
Tony: Yes. It is growing you.
Dr. Theo: Ah the growth – it does stretch us Tony, it's so tough sometimes. On a positive note, I just met someone else; another holistic doctor. I like her energy. Can you tell me about this person?
Tony: Yes. Visit her, she has a strong connection to the light. She will help you get back into your power professionally and personally.
Dr. Theo: Which therapy should I continue with her?
Tony: Have more of the sea water therapy.
Dr. Theo: Any wisdom for our life Tony?
Tony: Tend to one another. Trust in God, his will and your highest good.

Dr. Theo: Can we talk more often?
Tony: Yes. Via telepathy. Rest assured I am with you.
Dr. Theo: How can we REALLY hear you? Like… hear you hear you?
Tony: Depend on your abilities.
Dr. Theo: Can I use a tape recorder, as I can't bring a TV with me everywhere.
Tony: Yes. EVP.
Teresa: Tony, can I trust my co-worker? I feel she is sneaky.
Tony: No. She lies.
Teresa: Yes! She is a habitual liar! Thank you for the confirmation.
Dr. Theo: Tony is it in my highest good to work with the new social media manager I recently met?
Tony: No.
Dr. Theo: Please triple confirm with no.
Tony: No. No. No.
Dr. Theo: Thank you Tony.
Tony: Love and light, goodbye.

Saturday, July 8, 2017 6:15 PM
Spirit board session. Dr. Theo with his sister Teresa; Teresa's residence.

Dr. Theo states his affirmation invocation and the session begins.

Dr. Theo: Who is here with us today?
Unseen friend: Tony.
Teresa: Tony, why is it so difficult to date these days?
Tony: Dating gets ridiculous because no morals. People don't commit.
Dr. Theo: Tony, I will be going to Hawaii for a conference event and was thinking of taking the last girl I was dating but won't be now. Is it in my highest good to take someone else?
Tony: Not in your highest good. Though free will. Possibly meet someone there, but just be with nature. Be humble. Control ego.
Teresa: Why can't we get full sentences in EVP and just get few words at a time?
Tony: Can't. Frequency not on the same level. Can't stay on for long time.

Seconds go fast. 3 seconds max at this energy level to be in your fields.
Dr. Theo: So, I can call upon anyone I want to talk to me - anytime?
Tony: Whoever is available. Not everyone is available.
Dr. Theo: What are you all doing over there on that side? Does schooling continue with our consciousness in the other realms past death?
Tony: Such a very good question. Always growing and learning.
Dr. Theo: Why did you just answer this question so quickly? You must have really liked the question compared to our earlier ones.
Tony: Very Much! Just is. Smile from me.

At that very moment a humming bird appeared on the porch for thirty seconds. It sat still looking at us and then left! We were filled with joy!

Teresa: Tony did you just send the humming bird!?
Tony: You need nothing more than love. God always provides. Trust in God.
Teresa: Any more wisdom before we part from this session Tony?
Tony: Don't be discouraged, life is a learning curve.

Just as he said this, the humming bird returned and it flew in front of us, looked at us once more and then flew off! We were now so elated!

Dr. Theo: Wow! So very grateful for this amazing message today. Sending you lots of love and gratitude Tony.
Teresa: I love hummingbirds! Such a beautiful experience, goodbye Tony!
Tony: Much love, Good bye.

Monday, July 17, 2017 10:17 PM
Spirit Board session. Dr. Theo with his sister Teresa; Teresa's residence.

Dr. Theo states his affirmation invocation and the session begins.

Dr. Theo: Who is here with us today?
Unseen friend: Tony.
Teresa: Hello Tony!

Tony: So utterly depressed in people - Fatima.

The word 'Lady' came up on an EMF application I had running on my phone during the session. These programs are available for free as downloads online.

Teresa: Tony is talking about the anniversary this year of the 1917 Lady Fatima prophesy.
Tony: Yes.
Dr. Theo: Most people have not heeded anything to make them in general kinder or more loving.
Tony: No.
Teresa: Well that's people. Very slow to change.
Dr. Theo: Speaking of people and ascension. Tony, how long will it take our society to comfortably live with other alien races?
Tony: Many centuries.
Dr. Theo: Figures. Well, Tony I have the old school magnetic tape, handheld microcassette recorder you recommended I get. How do I use this thing to hear your voice and not have to use the board as much?
Tony: Turn on recorder. Ask question.
Dr. Theo: I have done that prior and have not heard anything. Just silence.
Tony: Takes time, do not rush, will learn in time.
Dr. Theo: So, when should I record and listen to it? Is there a time of day that would be best?
Tony: Often. Ask question, be patient and listen in the dead-spaced silence.
Dr. Theo: Are we still looking at the same time frame for the global economic change or has the frame shifted at all? What big event will occur before the collapse that will show us its coming? Will we be here in Los Angeles?
Tony: The banks will fail. It will be universal. You will travel back and forth from Los Angeles. Free will.
Dr. Theo: Well what would you have us do in that situation? Just sit and go through it?
Tony: Nothing to do. Love will show the way.
Dr. Theo: Okay, I'll try to relax about that. Onto a topic I love more, are all the steps I'm taking to show the works of healing going well - as planned -

from your view?
Tony: Yes! Do seminars.
Dr. Theo: Where should I do them?
Tony: All over the world.

At that point I got goosebumps, I had always felt intuitively that these seminars would be worldwide.

Dr. Theo: Will you help me? I need help to do this. There are people coming forward - is it in my highest good to connect with them to take everything further?
Tony: Yes. It will all show when time is right. You will know.
Dr. Theo: What is the ideal time to start them?
Tony: You will be given the sign.
Dr. Theo: Oh, come on Tony!
Tony: Life is a mystery. Smiley face.
Dr. Theo: Alright. Noted, thank you. So, I'd like to know more about this naturopath I met. I feel a past life connection and we are really helping each other grow. Can you tell me more? When, where and what? Any geographical data would be helpful also.
Tony: Friends who helped many people heal. Healers in war. 524 BC. Persia.
Dr. Theo: That is amazing, thank you. Any wisdom currently that you can give us for our lives at this present moment?
Tony: Be upbeat and happy always.
Teresa to **Dr. Theo:** Bro, let's hurry up and finish session I am so tired and I have to get up tomorrow for work early.
Tony: Realize the idea you are tired is only a thought.
Dr. Theo: Ha! That's so true, ok we're sending you lots of love and gratitude Tony.
Tony: With the utmost joy for you both, Good bye.

For the next session I decided to have two of my fellow student channels; Sonya and Melissa, from Shawn Randall's Thursday night class come to my office and work with spirit through the board, because all our connections to our guides were opening up. Both were excellent guests to accompany me on the board as we were all open to our guides and spiritual connection. Sonya and Melissa were both gifted in speaking with spirit in their own ways. Sonya, a fairy-like energy being, owns a pet care company and is a very empathic individual which is usually surrounded by unconditional loving energies, so that gives her an edge on tapping into the other side. Melissa, a lovely trusting and caring soul, had recently lost her fiancé. Her recent loss advanced her journey into a deeper spiritual connection. I felt our backgrounds would provide a productive session with interesting results. Indeed, it did.

Friday, July 28, 2017 8:15 PM
Classmates Sonya and Melissa with Dr. Theo on Spirit board at his office.

Dr. Theo states his affirmation invocation and the session begins. Quick connection with lots of energy.

Unseen friend: Hope.
Dr. Theo: Are you an angel from the light?
Unseen friend: Yes.
Dr. Theo: What is your name? Is it Hope?
Unseen friend: H t d e

Although the movement and energy were present, we weren't getting an actual name confirmation yet. It seemed the energy was having trouble slowing down its frequency in terms of matching words to signals.

Sonya: Are they having a hard time with the board?
Dr. Theo: No, there seems to be plenty of movement, maybe they're just having a tough time translating their name. It's not phonetically spelled the same between dimensions where it can make sense in our language - correct?
Unseen friend: Yes.
Dr. Theo: Okay well we will just refer to you as 'light of love', so what message do you bring us today?

Unseen friend: Hope, c h a v e c h o k 2
Sonya: I'm sorry, the only thing that made sense was hope, then it all seems garbled.
Unseen friend: E d w g o e p t f j d I o I o r Hope! Hope! Hope!
Dr. Theo: Dear friend, this doesn't make sense, you give us a bunch of letters then the word hope three times. We love you and thank you for the message of hope! We will say goodbye for now, thank you for being with us as we ask Tony to come through.

Dr. Theo: Who is here with us?
Unseen friend: Tony.
Dr. Theo: Excellent, Tony thank you for coming through. We are going to take a break and let Melissa and Sonya work with their guides.

At this time we switched positions, Sonya and Melissa took the board as I sat to write the incoming messages. Sonya states her affirmation invocation and the session continues. Indicator starts to move in circular pattern throughout the board, lots of energy, immediate connection.

Unseen friend: W I t h k e x s q u e s g s f s p f s p f r e [Unintelligible]
Melissa: What is your name?
Unseen friend: Muriel.
Dr. Theo: Your name is Muriel?
Muriel: Yes, Hello. Hope. N o w o d k [Unintelligible]
Sonya: Still seems we're getting codes. Are you the same entity as before?
Muriel: Yes, R f x c k o e I s k f z n e [Unintelligible]. Hope, hope evolves people, yes dear ones - love is the answer for humanity, yes, yes, yes. Down with suffering a f e n g I n g [Unintelligible] codes o e l o w e w p r e [Unintelligible] given to you yes, yes, yes, you yes, you yes. Hope Hope Hope, is universal code.
Dr. Theo: Does this have anything to do with the information Tony gave us about the future banking system failing? Is this about preparing for that event?
Muriel: No, No, No. All creation of reality possible. Yes, yes yes. No c l i p h c I t s [Unintelligible] hello, hello, hello, yes, hello, yes, no s e r v I s t o e r h

p h u w r y s f y I e w [Unintelligible] Goodbye!
Dr. Theo, Sonya and **Melissa:** Good bye Muriel!

The session was very energy erratic. Muriel however, delivered her clear message of hope! Sonya at this point had to get going to a later meeting so I wanted to be sure Melissa and her fiancé Emanuel on the other side had a change to communicate, so we put in a few more minutes to try to connect with him.

Dr. Theo: Emanuel, if you are available to speak to Melissa, please use this time to speak with her and give her your message.
Sonya: Yes, he's here, I can feel him pulling on my ponytail saying "You promised you would tell her I wanted to communicate with her." I have been feeling him talking to me on the way here earlier.
Melissa: That's him, he's very feisty and a lively energy!

Melissa states her affirmation invocation and the session continues.

Melissa: Emanuel, how are you doing there and do you have any advice for me in my life and future here?

Planchette starts to move, lots of energy, immediate connection.

Unseen friend: Hello, Yes, Emanuel, yes. Love grave to the grave f l I t o t m e [Unintelligible] my love Melissa yours o m g s [Unintelligible] at night. No love grander than k m I n [unintelligible], Hello U complete me, me, me, peaceful night to you my butterfly. Forever my heart Amen. Yes. Stay positive, I will meet you in your dreams, will dance my love, love w p u c l e k e k e k [unintelligible], Goodbye
Melissa: Goodbye my love! (sobbing) He called me his butterfly when he was in physical form, and we always kid about that old famous movie scene from Jerry MaGuire where we said that to each other the line, 'You complete me'. So sweet, the message. That was definitely him. I can tell he was getting through but with some challenge spelling the words.
Sonya: That was so beautiful, wow!

Dr. Theo: I very much agree.

After this amazing display of connecting with the disincarnate, I started gifting requests from acquaintances to help them also connect to their guides or departed ones. There were countless amazing experiences just as the one mentioned.

Thursday, August 3, 2017 7:30 PM
Spirit Board session. Dr. Theo with his sister Teresa at his residence.

Dr. Theo states his affirmation invocation and the session begins.

Dr. Theo: Who is here with us now?
Unseen friend: Tony. Very good to be here with you.
Teresa: Hello Tony!
Dr. Theo: Hello! Great to have you, as always Tony. So, I had a great time at a new radio interview today. I laughed when I heard the engineer's name there who I was introduced to was… Tony!
Tony: Yes. Good vibes with people.
Dr. Theo: Tony please tell me why opportunities seem to come out of nowhere.
Tony: Energy created thought.
Dr. Theo: Can you please elaborate?
Tony: Thoughts created your reality.
Dr. Theo: Excellent, yes please tell me more about this process! Any more wisdom on this?
Tony: Truth is within.
Dr. Theo: So now that I am moving forward with all this material that has channeled in, how can I bring it to the people so they receive it well?
Tony: Give it to them from the heart.
Dr. Theo: So, what is the ultimate truth?
Tony: Truth is love.
Dr. Theo: So, truth is within and it is love. We are this energy, which is love, or God? So, we all make up God?

Tony: You are a part of love. A child of God.

Dr. Theo: Thank you so much for that always comforting reminder. Speaking of within and heart matters, I have been getting some spurts of pain in my chest, which has me concerned. However, I feel it's blood flow, just certain body positioning causing the discomfort. Should I worry about this or is my intuition correct?

Tony: Nothing to worry about, it's nothing.

Dr. Theo: Thank you for the confirmation Tony. I am thinking of a new patient I am working with. I want to help her with her hearing loss and would like to know what her main block on healing is. I can offer her some new insight with your help. What message should I give her on her next visit in?

Tony: Fear not.

Dr. Theo: Yes, it seems that would be what is crippling her life. Overwhelming belief in fear.

Tony: Be a good listener.

Dr. Theo: I see, yes, she doesn't get much support in being allowed self-expression; she did mention not feeling like she's being heard. Incredible how this links together, thank you!

Tony: Yes.

Dr. Theo: How can we - all humanity - deal with the strong emotions and feelings of lust in physicality? It seems to be a rampant issue in society.

Tony: Seek with your soul, not your physical eyes.

Dr. Theo: You answered that quickly! Seems there are certain questions you like to really answer and others you're not so keen on. Which questions should we ask for better connection, like just now? And I have noticed it's a much better connection each time we communicate!

Tony: Self-growth questions. Goes faster as you go.

Dr. Theo: Makes perfect sense. So, I am trying to use the magnetic tape recorder you spoke about. I am talking into the air and leaving some silence between questions so you can answer. I have not yet heard any response yet. Why is this?

Tony: Must slow down the tape while listening to half speed.

Dr. Theo: I will keep trying the exercise, thank you for helping me understand this. How is my abundance thinking coming along? Any tips

you see from your side?
Tony: Yes, doing well. Keep as you are doing.
Dr. Theo: Excellent! Thank you. So where can I improve and be even better?
Tony: Look inside, find peace. Silence your mind.
Dr. Theo: Concerning our channeling practice, doing it solo and not in class where our energy is combined in unison, it's become quite challenging lately.
Tony: Must be practiced often, remove laziness. Be focused. No doubts.
Dr. Theo: True, I have been slacking lately.
Teresa: Yes, I admit also, it it's tough keeping on top of it. So many distractions, want to just be 'there' already. Why do some people already have the gift while others work so hard for small connections?
Tony: Not happening - doesn't work like that. Process is open to those who seek.
Dr. Theo: One last question for you Tony before we close for today. Are we good students, do you enjoy teaching us and answering our questions? Much love and gratitude to you Tony!
Tony: Yes! Good night, goodbye.

More Incredible Lessons

A year ago, my friend and patient John had come into my office for his usual therapy. At the end of his visit he was put on a rolling spinal traction unit which had him lying on his back and massaged his paraspinal muscles. When the visit concluded he left and went home. He called me frantically after he had checked his pockets and placed all his items on his bedroom dresser prior to turning in for the night. "I lost my angel coin at your office. I know I had it when I came in. I retraced my footsteps and I can't find it anywhere. Can you please check to see if it fell under, inside or on the side of the roller table against the wall for me?" I checked everywhere, top to bottom inside and outside the machine. I called him back with the sad news that I didn't find it and suggested he may have lost it in his car seat or it fell in the car console as things usually do fall in there. He assured he had checked there too and was sure it was lost while he was relaxing on the machine. After a recent session with John on the spirit board talking with Tony in my office, a miracle occurred for John that confirmed his belief in the process of communication with his own light guides and angels. He had a firm belief that he was very connected to his passed-over parents, especially his mother - who he swears loves to push the elevator buttons for him at his office building, without him needing to! So, John called me the weekend after his board session where he had the opportunity to speak with Tony about some business choices he was making at the time. The following is what he told me on that call:

"I had just gotten out of the shower with a towel wrapped around my waist. I heard some text messages come in that I wanted to get to quickly. I dried off my hair and tucked the towel securely around my hips as I grabbed my cell phone from the sink counter and walked into the living room typing back the texts. I sat down on a leather chair to collect my thoughts while typing. As I sat there (still half dried and half still wet) from my front left periphery I saw something shiny come out from the ceiling and crash down to the floor with a loud thud. I stood up and walked forward towards the object that just seemed to go directly to the floor without rolling or skipping. It just went straight from the celling to the floor and stopped. As I stood up to investigate what this was, I was amazed and in disbelief that it was the angel coin I lost at your office over a year ago! I checked everywhere around me, there was nowhere in the chair that the coin could have been lodged in. I saw an object come from in front of me. I'm also fully naked with just a towel around me, so I didn't have it on me or in any pockets! This is incredible, you must ask Tony for me, what happened? Where was the coin all this time? How did this just appear out of thin air? I'm at a loss for words and shaking! I can't talk to others about this, they'll think I'm crazy!"

Of course, I was very intrigued about what I just had heard. It reminded me of my experience with the manifested rose petal which appeared also out of nowhere right in front of my patient as I concluded teaching her about removing negative thoughts. I had to ask Tony about this in my next session...

Wednesday, August 9, 2017 8:25 PM
Spirit Board session. Dr. Theo with his sister Teresa; Dr. Theo's office.

Dr. Theo states his affirmation invocation and the session begins.

Dr. Theo: Thank you for connecting, who is here with us?
Unseen friend: Tony. Hello!
Dr. Theo and **Teresa:** Hello Tony!
Dr. Theo: Tony we really appreciate the beautiful connection and communication you are sharing with us to empower our spiritual journey. Life is definitely much more interesting and smoother with your help. I am thinking of a patient and concerned for her well-being. She has left overseas and has yet to be in communication about how she is doing. Can you offer any insight as to what is going on with her life at this time? How can I help more?
Tony: She is having family issues. Youngest child and has a hard time with monetary things. She has a commitment with you and she honors that.
Dr. Theo: So, to help her, I can offer her a discount or offer to cut her costs to help her further?
Tony: Yes.
Dr. Theo: Thank you for the insight Tony. I must ask about the coin that John told me he was given back that appeared out of nowhere - thin air. He claims the coin dropped from the ceiling and fell to the floor as he sat in his living room chair. He swears it was the same angel coin that went missing over a year ago in my office. He says it didn't come out of his pockets or dislodge from anywhere. How did this physical coin materialize like this a year later?
Tony: His guides dropped it.
Dr. Theo: What!? From where!? How!?
Tony: Hollow time. Most lifetimes are connected through hollow time.
Dr. Theo: Please tell us about hollow time!

I quickly searched online 'hollow time' on my smart phone and got nothing.

Tony: You need more knowledge, can't understand.

Dr. Theo: Try me! Can you please tell me so I can understand? This is very fascinating, I need to learn this!
Tony: Humans in this lifetime will never know. Death from this life will open the veil.
Dr. Theo: Ok, so it's not yet in our collective consciousness to know this information at this time. It would be like telling a caveman what email is. They don't even understand electricity or computers, so explaining email is useless. Let's move onto the next question then. Can you please tell me if the woman who came in today and learned about her energy field was pleased with the life-changing information she received?
Tony: Yes, she is appreciating of the help.

The same patient emailed me later that night saying the same thing and thanking me for her healing session.

Dr. Theo: Thank you Tony. As you of course know, I was rear-ended last night by a driver who was on her cell phone. The driver had no insurance, no plates on her Prius, and no registration. The police never showed up. She gave me her phone number and said she would text me her insurance information once she got home and found it. Of course, she didn't respond later when I asked her politely to send it via text. I went to the police station the next day and after waiting to be seen for two hours, they wouldn't help me at all. There is about $1,300 of paint damage to my bumper. Please tell me why did I have to go through this random and seemingly inconvenient experience? I was minding my own business at a stopped red light.
Tony: Let love guide you. Things like these don't matter. Don't stress.
Dr. Theo: Though why do I feel like a victim here? I can forgive her negligence, I am doing my best to do so. Where is the cosmic justice?
Tony: Your perception, [not you] is that of a victim. Be positive.
Dr. Theo: Thank you for that clarification, yes, I see your point. Faster I let it go, faster I move on from the lesson or challenge that I am presented with. That this our only true growth. These things test our perception.
Tony: Yes!
Dr. Theo: I always enjoy our sessions Tony. Please tell our guides we love them as I know they are always with us. Tony, any words of wisdom for us

before we depart tonight?
Tony: Yes. Keep smiling. Life is a gift, goodbye.
Dr. Theo and **Teresa:** Thank you Tony, till next time, goodbye!

After that, three weeks pass by between the last connection with the spirit world and returning to channeling class. Much happened during that time including hearing from a colleague of mine that was caught in the middle of Hurricane Harvey in Texas. I was on a trip to Hawaii for a business convention held there for a week. I went on the trip solo and it was quite peaceful and self-reflective. While there I decided to find joy in nature like Tony had suggested, but I also made a request to have fun with someone of like mind. I met an attractive lady on the last day there. I asked about this and the manifestation process on my next session with Heroditus.

Thursday, August 31, 2017 5:05 PM
Spirit Board session. Dr. Theo and Shawn; Shawn's office. Recorded session.

Shawn: We surround this board with love and light and only those with the highest wisdom, truth and love are invited here. We open to those who are in Theo's highest good.

Dr. Theo: Heroditus! (Laughing)
Shawn: With a special request for Heroditus. (Laughing)

Planchette starts to move throughout the board, lots of energy, immediate connection.

Unseen friend: Dear one I am here - Heroditus. At your service.
Shawn: I can feel him; he is down-stepping his energy.
Heroditus: For you Theo are deeply loved. Question?
Dr. Theo: Heroditus as you know, we now going through national pain with Hurricane Harvey ripping through Texas, and I have an old classmate and colleague there who has lost everything. Was there a particular reason for this hurricane and why do 'natural' disasters that claim so many lives happen?

Heroditus: There are many reasons for disasters at this time. Now 'Harvey' awakens compassion at a time when perspectives and values have grown out of perspective. Frivolous thinking such as 'fake news' obsessions are now in a perspective allowing the human heart to shine mass consciousness.

Dr. Theo: So, is this mass consciousness causing the lessons each person involved in the disaster chose, or is this an act of God throwing down peril on the people?

Heroditus: Mass consciousness of an unconscious kind. The collective unconscious pushes its shadow upward in order that human-kind grows in wisdom. This is an integration process spanning humanity's entire history.

Dr. Theo: So, for instance, the tragedy of September 11th, 2011 (or 9/11) was the same thing?

Heroditus: Exactly, same with the exception of the arrival of the visual 'terrorist' for the first time.

Dr. Theo: I had a relative who was on the 104th floor of the North Tower. She died on 9/11 and since then, it's difficult to believe any 'official' explanations. Please explain the government's inside job aspect of involvement.

Heroditus: Inside what? Not completely. It is all the same pool of human consciousness. Blame and blaming slows awareness from dawning. Power is in awareness and choice. Humanity needs more of both! The invasions resulted: however, the collateral damage was not intended at the level done. It does not serve you Theo to think of the world and humanity as forces of conspiracy vs. the powerless masses. The reality is far more complex. Seek the complexity; otherwise you will become susceptible to theories put forth by those with selfish agendas.

Shawn: I'm getting a picture he's saying that being focused into forced righteousness can cause you to pick a side that makes you wanting to become right, and hold onto resentment towards certain forces; He's saying it won't serve you to stay in that vibration.

Dr. Theo: I do understand why he explains this the way he does. And I understand that being focused on certain one-sided details takes focus away from the bigger lesson to be learned. Heroditus, an entity named 'Tony' has been coming through the board a lot, and the messages he shares with my sister and I are powerful. Can you tell me about Tony and our interactions? We haven't heard from our other personal guides since we started channeling class, and I'm wondering why?

Shawn: So, you haven't had your personal guides come through and only Tony, the light being - not your Uncle Tony - has been teaching you on the board? Have you done spirit board work with others as well?

Dr. Theo: Yes, I have with some other individuals who wanted guidance and we received guidance with Tony coming through to help provide answers. Depending on the energy mix of the person I pair up with and myself, the energy and flow seems to be faster with those who are open fearless believers, and slower with those who are not. Our connection here is moving at lightning speed. Heroditus comes through a lot when the vibratory frequency is highest.

Shawn: Yes, yes. Honored he is here with us.

Dr. Theo: As am I. My question to you Heroditus is, where have my four primary guides Ariadne, Exter, Joy, and Devous been all this time? They haven't come in channel or the board since I've started this wonderful awakening.

Heroditus: Energy 'Tony' is a loving well intending being in 'training' to become a master teacher. His strength is teaching you about you and your 'truth' relative to the source. Ask questions relative to this.

Dr. Theo: Unseen friend Tony tells us he is from a place of light, an energy form, the same place our Uncle Tony is at now. The light energy took on our Uncle Tony's name for familiarity and identification while working with us.

Shawn: That's great! Makes sense. Sounds right to me.

Dr. Theo: So, energy or unseen friend Tony is earning his wings! (Laughter)

Heroditus: He loves to help others in ways that empower.

Shawn: Is that true? Do you feel empowered after the sessions?

Dr. Theo: Oh yes. He always provides great information and is loving. We can feel his energy in the room, amazing. He's even sent a humming bird to us!

Heroditus: We give him the space on the board with you to evolve and grow, however, focus mostly for you and I to grow intimacy in our relationship and deep trust. This is important.

Dr. Theo: I know that working with you Heroditus in my practice, personal

life, and doing the channeling has brought me tremendous growth. How am I doing with my channeling process from your point of view?
Heroditus: Doing quite well yet be aware of trusting yourself and me, your guide [the connection], more than Tony. Focus on healing work.
Shawn: So, it's a little bit of a head's up. Maybe Theo you're putting too much attention to the work with Tony, while you should focus on your connection to you and your guides as creator and co-creator.
Dr. Theo: I do my best to stay neutral, I don't want to play favorites. I am aware that they are all here for my higher good and I am growing quickly in my journey as a healer! Just in the short time of a year I've catapulted. I feel the energy and messages I am given, and if it serves me in a positive manner I use it. I feel Heroditus is asking me to be aware with the placement of my power and attention. I do understand his loving council.
Shawn: That's good.
Dr. Theo: So, I would like to ask Heroditus, how am I doing from your side of the veil in terms of prosperity thinking? What baggage do I still need to drop, to get to my next level of higher awareness?
Heroditus: Drop ALL, ALL, ALL - blame of anyone and anything.
Shawn: That is a big one to contemplate.
Dr. Theo: Heroditus, please give me specifics.
Heroditus: Blame of situations, parts of yourself, obstacles you perceive as from someone else, and conditions such as 'astrology'.
Shawn: He's meaning that no matter what, be free of it. Such as blaming parents, the weather, astrology (mercury retrogrades), traffic conditions, or circumstances that may not go your way. Etc. etc.
Dr. Theo: Yes, just be free of everything so all good possibilities may come! All thoughts of attachment and blame keep us from expanding to other better possibilities and limit our receptivity of good.
Heroditus: Yes. Yes! Focus on your creator-self and your co-creator sources.
Shawn: So Heroditus, that would include him, his higher self, his guides, you Heroditus, Christ consciousness, angels, archangels, God, Goddess or all that is. Correct?
Heroditus: Indeed.
Dr. Theo: So, speaking of co-creating, who helped bring that beautiful woman to the surf shop when I was in Hawaii? I wanted to share the last

day of my trip with someone fun and attractive. I just asked in my mind, and low and behold, I went surfing that morning with someone nice. We had fun surfing the whole morning. We then went to lunch and spent more time together. She was even from the same location as I was from back home in Los Angeles. It was pretty amazing super synchronicity. I couldn't help but laugh and be grateful knowing you all had a part in making that happen.

Heroditus: Your guides and hers collaborated - and I was a part of it too!

Dr. Theo: Yes, I thought so. And on that note, is it possible to enjoy the physicality of each other without negative repercussions or feelings getting hurt, so that both can benefit from the positive energy exchange, leaving both intimately fulfilled?

Heroditus: Yes, it is possible with honesty and clarity with self and sharing that with someone who is not 'needy' and unaware of creating their reality.

Shawn: And one must also be aware of the shadow or lower energy version of self, which could be activated and integrate into the equation.

Dr. Theo: Our society is moving toward gender equality and issues of the transgender sex. Religious leaders seem to not be helping, adding blame and confusion on the topic. Are spirits from your side sexless - do they choose during birth to be born gay, transgender or straight - so much confusion about this and God's part in all of it. Can you clarify this for us?

Heroditus: Yes, gender issues are chosen unconsciously by the soul and higher-self prior to incarnation. The choice is always there. However, the issue of living from one's true self including gender dynamics must be dealt with one way or another. God has no judgement and allows this very creative growth process.

Dr. Theo: So, what about those who grow in environments which persuade or encourage someone to belong to a homosexual or transgender identity. Some do choose to live as a gay man or lesbian woman. There are instances where a man who is straight grows up with all feminine influence, no male role models and ends up wearing his mother's clothes, cosmetics and high heels growing up, fantasizing being like his mother. This does occur; can you explain this scenario?

Heroditus: It would be an act, however if they convince themselves "I used to love gin but now I choose to love vodka instead," that person must never see gin again or be reminded of it, otherwise there will be conflict of the heart.

Dr. Theo: Ah, I understand. This is where the inner turmoil and deep personal struggle lies; this is where people suffer about their true sexual identity, feeling isolated, different, confused, exiled and unloved. Indeed, this must feel like a living Hell when they reach out to their religious leaders for advice. They don't get a loving explanation, but instead rebuked - because the priest, rabbi or pastor has no clue how to help with compassion for how and what they're feeling.

Shawn: I know a few straight men over the years who have chosen a gay lifestyle. Are they fully happy? Not sure. But this does bring clarity. Now, some scientists are saying there are genes possibly linked to sexual orientation, but the big questions remain if it is inheritable. We have to close the session unfortunately as we are running out of time and I have to start the channeling class; this has been very insightful information Heroditus, thank you.

Heroditus: Love your curiosity and you Theo, Goodbye.

Dr. Theo: Thank you, goodbye Heroditus!

Tuesday, September 5, 2017 8:30 PM
Spirit Board session. Dr. Theo with his sister Teresa; Teresa's residence.

Dr. Theo states his affirmation invocation and the session begins.

Dr. Theo: Who is here with us helping and guiding us through our journey today?

Unseen friend: Tony.

Teresa: Hello Tony!

Dr. Theo: Hello Tony. So Heroditus says you are learning by helping us, to get your masters! That's excellent! So, there's a schooling system on the other side as there is here?

Tony: Every ending has a new beginning. All souls grow.

Dr. Theo: Wait, so you were a human at one time?

Tony: No. I am from the source, a light energy.

Dr. Theo: So even though you were not a human with a past life, you still

grow in your own way as energy?
Tony: Yes.
Dr. Theo: Very interesting. So, do all soul energies come from God?
Tony: Yes.
Dr. Theo: So, some energies that come from the source Creator, choose to become humans and some don't?
Tony: Yes. Some choose incarnation on a planet or none at all.
Dr. Theo: So how many lifetimes have I incarnated on Earth?
Tony: Many.
Dr. Theo: So as an old soul, can you give me the number of lifetimes?
Tony: No not important. Focus on now.
Dr. Theo: How about my sister; is she from another planet? Is she 'out of this world'? Ha! (Laughing)
Tony: Yes Venus.
Teresa: Don't you know men are from Mars and women are from Venus?
Tony: Ha – Ha – Ha –Ha.
Dr. Theo: Tony, come on! Seriously? Her soul has previously incarnated on Venus?
Tony: No. But some have. Choice.
Dr. Theo: Okay, new topic; a health question. My left foot is swollen from walking on the beach on Labor Day and I have no idea what I stepped on but it stung and felt deep. Will I be okay? It's starting to look bad, hope it's not infected. Why did this happen, I was having a good day and this randomly happened!
Tony: A sharp edge of a shell piece.
Dr. Theo: Ah, good to know it wasn't some hypodermic needle. I don't like the dark ocean water here.
Tony: You will be okay. It happened because of a lack of faith.
Dr. Theo: Wow. Yes, I was telling my friend I was with, how I didn't trust the beaches in California, so I don't go swimming in the ocean here, unlike the clear Caribbean or Mediterranean waters. It was incredible right when it happened a very nice girl came up to me and brought me water to clean off my wound and a sterile bandage; what a coincidence she would have these things with her!?
Tony: No. Not a coincidence. Nothing is coincidence.

Dr. Theo: Oh, I stand corrected, yes, that's right - it's all divinely planned by thoughts in motion.
Tony: Yes.
Dr. Theo: So where is Heroditus when I am channeling by myself, outside of class? I feel he's not coming through like he does when I am in class, where I feel his energy much stronger. Why is that?
Tony: Meditation. You need to meditate more often and deeper.
Teresa: Tony I have a question about sex. My mother keeps telling me sex before marriage is a bad thing and a sin, is this true?
Tony: No. Sex is natural.
Teresa: So, when is it bad?
Tony: When done for selfish reasons. Sin is a lack of love.
Dr. Theo: So, when expressed with someone you love it is blessed and good?
Tony: Yes.
Dr. Theo: That makes total sense; the Church has twisted this to make people feel guilt so it can control.
Tony: Yes.
Dr. Theo: Can you tell me what is going on with my co-host? We're supposed to start a radio show and there's a lack of proper communication between us lately, it makes me nervous as I really like solid organization.
Tony: Other things on her mind.
Dr. Theo: When we start will this be a productive, fun and prosperous venture?
Tony: Yes. If you both choose.
Dr. Theo: Tony thank you so much, as always you make things brighter and bring us clarity in life's little road bumps. With much gratitude, we say farewell for now.
Tony: Thank you, my pleasure, love and light goodbye.

Thursday, September 7th, 2017 4:00 PM
Dr. Theo and Shawn; Shawn's office. Spirit Board Recorded session.

Shawn: We surround this board and ourselves with love and light and only those with the highest wisdom, truth and love are invited here. We open to those who are in Theo's highest good, with a special request for Theo's healer guide Heroditus to join us.

Planchette indicator moves immediately for connection.

Heroditus: Yes, now I am with you. Let's begin.
Dr. Theo: Thank you for being with us Heroditus. I feel I have really worked on my prosperity thinking and am making progress on how I process through the events in my life. Since writing the books I see my patients also benefiting from the experiences and tools I share with them. Can you please give me a structure of thinking that can catapult this work into massive abundance? As my guide, what do you propose would be the best personal action plan for me?
Shawn: Yes, this is a very good question!
Heroditus: Dear Theo, begin each day feeling prosperous. Allow your lingering 'dreamy' state to be consciously directed to prosperity resonance and beliefs… so that you feel great and start the day off on the right… not foot …wallet!
Shawn: How clever! (Laughing)
Dr. Theo: (Laughing) Thank you Heroditus, this is very good information. How about throughout my day?
Heroditus: Use your favorite affirmations from a list you construct as you go through your day feeling great as you do so.
Dr. Theo: And for the end of my day?
Heroditus: Write a short gratitude list of prosperity events that happened throughout the day to you. Ask for prosperity dreams and that your higher-self join you and co-create prosperity with you. Ask for help!
Dr. Theo: Thank you so much for that Heroditus - it helps me so much! Gratitude!
Shawn: Very good advice! The subconscious will get the message from the gratitude list and you can go into the dream state continually creating on gratitude, thus attracting more.
Dr. Theo: Yes, yes - Excellent! Heroditus can you please help me naturally default to positive thinking?
Heroditus: Deal with all your fears.

Dr. Theo: How exactly? That's easier said than done sometimes - deep seated fears are so elusive. I would like to incorporate more healing into my methods.
Shawn: Heroditus, how specifically can he remove his fears regarding prosperity?
Heroditus: Remember they are only stories… and as trash bags… send them away as you would an annoying bug.
Shawn: I love that! That's great! Ha! He didn't say squash the bug though.
Dr. Theo: How long would this manifestation process take?
Heroditus: Must give it at least 72 hours and at the most 3 weeks.
Shawn: When can he feel an expansion of prosperity happening if Theo incorporates everything mentioned?
Heroditus: 3 to 4 weeks.
Dr. Theo: Not long at all! Thank you - yes! On another note, my father is having some difficulty with property management overseas. Is the property in jeopardy?
Heroditus: Inappropriate question.
Shawn: You are a secondary co-creator; this may be a question about your father's life and his prosperous creating of reality (or lack there-of). So Heroditus is hinting for you to focus on your own abundance. Perhaps a practical talk with your father on these and spiritual matters may help him turn the prosperity tide in his favor. It would also help in his thinking of health matters also since he is up in age.
Dr. Theo: Speaking of getting older and health, Heroditus should I be concerned with the feelings I am getting in my chest/heart or is this just positional? Is what was found on MRI something to be concerned about or will my body take care of it by itself? Can you scan me now and let me know if there are any health issues I should be aware of?
Heroditus: Continue as you are doing and add strong positive beliefs you feel daily.
Shawn: It may be a good idea to add this to your prosperity meditation that Heroditus just mentioned earlier.
Heroditus: You are healthy!
Dr. Theo: Thank you for that reassurance Heroditus.
Shawn: We have time for one more question in this session.

Dr. Theo: I am changing my practice to more mind and spiritual work; less physical. Any hints/help?
Heroditus: Yes! Excellent! I heartily agree! Add it all together. Keep the practice!
Shawn: We're out of time and we must say goodbye for now.
Heroditus: We must go - Goodbye and thank you!
Dr. Theo: Thank you so much Heroditus!
Shawn: Good bye Heroditus!

Sunday, Sept 17, 2017 9:30 PM
Spirit Board session. Dr. Theo with his sister Teresa; Teresa's residence.

Dr. Theo states his affirmation invocation and the session begins.

Dr. Theo: Who is here now guiding us through our journey?
Unseen friend: Tony here. Hello my students, what a glorious day!
Dr. Theo and Teresa: Hi Tony!
Tony: God loves you with all his might.
Teresa: Right back from us! I have a question about praying to certain saints and finding things immediately. I pray to St. Mina and I find things I lost immediately. I also pray to St. Fanourio, both saints of lost items, and they help me find things. It seems the things I lost find me back! How does this happen?
Tony: Energy. Energy depends on how ready they are to receive your request and return items.
Dr. Theo: How much longer will you be with us Tony?
Tony: A while longer. Why do you not like my teaching?
Dr. Theo: That's not why I ask. I know that some guides come in and others go out, I was wondering about how long you will be teaching us. So, what other wisdom can you impart on us today in this session?
Tony: Ask.
Dr. Theo: Ah yes, if we don't ask we don't receive.
Teresa: I have a question, how about this: Are there any of our relatives that have passed over, have any messages for us?
Dr. Theo: Good question!
Tony: Yes, grandfather; your father's side. He has a message for your father,

his son.

Dr. Theo: That's our Grandpa Teddy, Theodore. Same first name as me. A message for our dad? What is it?

Tony: He wants you to tell your father he is sorry for listening to his daughters, his sisters.

Dr. Theo: Yes grandpa, I and my siblings never really got to know you - you were never around.

Tony: He says, "Your aunts - your father's sisters - kept him away from your family. They controlled with guilt."

Teresa: Yes, they were mean hearted. One of them is on the other side, one is still here on this side. I remember, very bitter and mean.

Tony: He says, "Daughter on my side is learning slowly. Daughter on earth; she will get her lesson."

Dr. Theo: Grandpa, what did you see when you passed?

Tony: He says, "Unconditional love."

Teresa: Thank you Grandpa, is there anyone else Tony that wants to speak with us for other messages?

Tony: Yes. Polimgia. Your mother's mother. Your grandmother.

Dr. Theo: Wow, spelled out her name perfectly! What is her message?

Tony: Her daughters need to make up and forgive each other.

Teresa: Oh yeah right, that's not going to happen anytime soon Tony. Too much pride and jealousy.

Tony: Very sad.

Teresa: Yes indeed, anyone else there Tony?

Tony: Yes, your Uncle Tony.

Teresa: Yay Uncle Tony! What is our uncle's message?

Tony: He says, "I miss life."

Dr. Theo: Well we miss you so much, but you can always incarnate again.

Tony: He says, "No. I love it here."

Dr. Theo: (Laughing) I don't blame you Uncle Tony. But do tell me what is your fondest moment while here with us?

Tony: He says, "Restaurant memories. And the fan incident."

Dr. Theo: (Laughing) Oh boy, you won't let that up, will you? I know, I know. Dumb thing to do, kids are kids.

Tony: He says, "That was hilarious."

Dr. Theo: Yes, it was, but for me also a painful lesson. (Laughing) Thank you Uncle Tony, we love you, you will always be in our heart and mind.
Tony: He says he loves you also and goodbye.
Dr. Theo: Okay so upon time of death, can the body or ego make the soul stay on this earth or is the soul in charge?
Tony: No. The soul has the last say.
Dr. Theo: But we have free will, can't we prolong the stay?
Tony: Yes, if one's will is strong enough.
Teresa: So, if free will exists, is it bad to kill oneself through suicide then?
Tony: Yes, soul is in turmoil. Life is a gift.
Dr. Theo: So when the soul consciousness goes fully to the Other Side and sees all the possibilities that were still available to get out of the challenges here, and realizes that the choice of taking its life was the worst choice, it puts itself into a cycle of pain, regret and feeling resentment for the decision made?
Tony: Exactly.
Dr. Theo: So God is not tormenting the soul, it's the soul itself feeling it didn't complete its mission or purpose it set out to do; it sees the chance it had and that it messed up its own plan to experience or carry out their time here. And similarly, if one wants to leave this life, he (or she) can ask for circumstances to occur to be taken out naturally.
Tony: Yes.
Dr. Theo: Great confirmation Tony, thank you.
Teresa: We're yawning and getting tired, it's late now so I think we should continue another time. Goodnight Tony.
Dr. Theo: I think you are right. Goodnight!
Tony: Go to bed. Love and light, goodbye.

Friday, September 22, 2017 10:34 PM
Spirit Board session. Dr. Theo with his sister Teresa; Dr. Theo's residence.

Dr. Theo states his affirmation invocation and the session begins.

Dr. Theo: Who is here with us?
Unseen friend: Tony.

Dr. Theo: Tony hello, how are you?
Tony: Fine.
Dr. Theo: No, really - you can feel emotions?
Tony: Yes, how you do.
Dr. Theo: You can feel sad, happy and the various feelings we feel; the whole range? Do you feel sad or mad ever?
Tony: Yes, whole range. Though sad and mad are on the other side.
Dr. Theo: You mean Hell or the vibrations of less than love?
Tony: Yes. D l r n w t r [Unintelligible]

Planchette shifts speed and moves with slower connection. Words not making much sense.

Dr. Theo: Tony what is going on with the energy, there is little movement.
Tony: Drink more water.
Dr. Theo: Who, both of us?
Tony: Theo.
Dr. Theo: Why? Is it because I drank some wine after dinner about 30 minutes ago before this session?
Tony: Yes.
Teresa: Let's both drink up!
Dr. Theo: Okay, drank a lot. Two glasses of water. Tony how do I look now?
Tony: OK.
Dr. Theo: Oh, I see, my body had to dilute alcohol as it was interfering with the signal of transmission not allowing our connection to be strong. This is what happens when people use drugs and alcohol, changes the frequency dial and they cannot be aware for their psychic connection or worse even – they may invite unwanted malicious energies in!
Tony: Yes, exactly.

Connection improves and speeds up again.

Dr. Theo: Wow - Great to see this in 'reality'. Just one glass of wine can really lower the ability to connect on a high vibe with you. Our connection now is much stronger, we're receiving information quicker. So, I'm so curious - what is Heaven like Tony? I know we asked this before, but can

you tell us more?
Tony: Unexplainable. It's glorious.
Dr. Theo: How does one get to Heaven?
Tony: Be of the light the life and the truth.
Teresa: So good people always go to Heaven?
Tony: Depends.
Dr. Theo: On what?
Tony: Deeds.
Teresa: Like a more good than bad scale?
Tony: Love your neighbor.
Dr. Theo: Is there a life 'review' when we die? Who reviews our lives with us? How long does it take?
Tony: Yes. Your guardian angels. Takes seconds, however your religions assign linear 'time' to it.
Teresa: What's next after the life review?
Tony: The soul sees both Heaven and Hell. Then it goes to one or the other depending on deeds.
Dr. Theo: Is the soul there for eternity, or does it feel like forever because there is no 'time' on that side? If one truly repents and loved ones pray for the soul to be lifted, does it move vibrationally out of the negativity?
Tony: No does not stay forever. Yes, lifted out by angels, if truly repents.
Dr. Theo: I saw this shown to me in a vision. When we are not creating positively, we imprison our own soul in turmoil. It seems the world has always been in flux when indifferent to God and his message. God does speak to humanity; seems we just don't listen.
Tony: Signs are already happening but people are not listening. All is possible when with God.
Dr. Theo: Tony, when we sleep where do we go? Our body stays in this reality, but where do 'we' go?
Tony: Right into the dream state.
Teresa: We don't go over to your side, same place you're at?
Tony: No.
Dr. Theo: Can you please tell us more about the dream state?
Tony: No. It is not important for your growth at this time. It is also a great mystery.

Teresa: Are dreams 'real'? I had Déjà vu is that real?
Tony: No dreams are not real. This is all relative.
Dr. Theo: So where is the soul actually while we sleep? Isn't there a place?
Tony: No, it is between dimensions.
Dr. Theo: Thank you Tony. Figures - it is getting late and we're just getting to the juicy questions! We will continue another time.
Teresa: Thank you so much, goodbye!
Tony: Light and love, goodbye!

Sunday, October 23, 2017 9:45 PM
Spirit Board session. Dr. Theo with his sister Teresa; Teresa's residence.

Dr. Theo states his affirmation invocation and the session begins.

Dr. Theo: Who is here with us?
Unseen friend: Tony.
Dr. Theo: Tony hello!
Teresa: Tony we felt called to ask guidance as it has been a very stressful week. My colleagues at the hospital and I are picketing this week at work, is a strike coming also? We're all very unhappy at work, our raises have been withheld from us for the last year and the excuses we're being given aren't adding up.
Tony: The strike is inevitable. Management is lying and lining its pockets.
Teresa: Yes, that's what we all thought too!
Dr. Theo: That's pretty sad. People are capable of great feats, but also can bear very negative energy. Speaking of negative energy and negative intent; I have to thank with much gratitude, all of my guides for the loving tap on the shoulder and the whisper in my ear this past weekend. I had a quick meetup with someone I spontaneously met on Friday. Very low energy.
Tony: She is a con artist. She extorts people. Delete her from your life. God balances inequalities.
Dr. Theo: What a sad soul; hopefully she turns her life around before it's too late. Thank you so much for your help and guidance. Unbelievable gratitude.
Tony: I am always with you.

Dr. Theo: Today is quite a day of revelation. While on the topic of work and business, my friend asked me to inquire about his investment ventures. He has several offers. He wants to line up with the highest good for his company's future and I'd like to help him if you have any words of wisdom.
Tony: Be cautious of the ones who rush him. Follow his gut. Free will.
Dr. Theo: Any advice on my patient with the disorderly children? How can I best help her?
Tony: Listen.
Dr. Theo: Ah yes, the ever powerful 'lend an ear' technique.
Teresa: I have questions about my new puppy, Cupid! How is he doing and is this milk formula okay for him or not, it seems to be bloating him too much.
Tony: Cupid is a ball of love. No more milk. Do not give it to him.
Teresa: Thank you Tony, I felt it was irritating his stomach.
Dr. Theo: How about chicken?
Tony: Yes, but boiled first.
Teresa: Thank you!
Dr. Theo: Tony, with so much chaos going on in our world; racism, sexism, America vs. Russia, North Korea, China, the presidency, politics, etc., everything seems so nutty. What is the dark side's ultimate goal for America?
Tony: Civil war. All over the world, not just America.
Dr. Theo: Who is pushing this to happen? Is it the global elite families who wish to maintain the status quo, those hiding free energy from the masses and depressing true human evolution?
Tony: Yes, the 'rich'. They want a New World Order.
Dr. Theo: Is this where they wish to manipulate people with microchips, just as the Bible prophecy warns; that no man will be able to buy, sell or trade without the mark of the beast in their right hand or forehead?
Tony: Yes. They have already started to push the agenda.
Dr. Theo: So, are the banks going to come down before the civil war?
Tony: Civil war will be first attempt then the bank collapse. All possibilities.
Dr. Theo: Yes, I know that we all have free will and mass consciousness tips the scale towards the things that come to fruition. So, these horrible things don't have to all happen correct?

Tony: Yes, correct.
Dr. Theo: Can we do something to keep them from occurring or is this all destined to happen; what can I do to do my part?
Tony: Pray.
Dr. Theo: Amen. So, Tony, is there really a population control agenda in the works under the guise of public health and safety?
Tony: Yes.
Dr. Theo: God help us all then. The most important thing for each of us is our own connection with Source Creator. How am I doing with my meditations in the last week?
Tony: Good.
Dr. Theo: I still have yet to experience my next big breakthrough Tony, when is this coming?
Tony: Takes time.
Dr. Theo: Is there anything else I need to know for my spiritual evolution?
Tony: Yes, focus.

At this time we were both fatigued and had no further questions. Tony knew this and after thirty seconds of inactivity the planchette moved straight to goodbye.

Tony: Goodbye.
Dr. Theo and **Teresa:** Goodbye Tony. Thank you!

Thursday, November 09, 2017 8:45 PM
Leona, Dr. Theo and Shawn in Shawn's channeling class. Board session.

Shawn Randall sat with another classmate, Leona, communicating with her and her spirit guide using the spirit board while I scribed the messages coming in. The objective here was to see if Leona's spirit guide could keep their focus on communication if I sat in on the board session with Leona instead of Shawn.

Dr. Theo sits in chair as Leona enters from right, Shawn exists chair to left.

Classmate's unseen friend: V a n a y h o n e y m a x o x o [Unintelligible]

Dr. Theo: Maybe I should ask my guide Heroditus to come through and help clear this up?
Shawn: Yes, say your affirmation invocation and bring in energy Tony or your healer guide Heroditus.

Dr. Theo states his affirmation invocation and the session continues.

Unseen friend: W a t a v e x b y o x [Unintelligible]
Dr. Theo: Who is here with us?
Unseen friend: Y a l a l a l n [Unintelligible]
Dr. Theo: That is not making any sense - are you with the light?
Unseen friend: Yes.
Dr. Theo: So what is your name?
Unseen friend: H a b o t l v u [Unintelligible]

The energy seemed to feel like he was trying to hint it was Heroditus.

Dr. Theo: This happens whenever I do a session with a new person. It seems it takes a while to connect with the new person and get a clear rhythmic connection. However, with my sister or you Shawn it's immediate and I can use the board to communicate without a problem. Some seem to have difficulty, like this right now is frustrating. We have a very fast connection, but it's not at all clear.

Shawn: Let me take the board again with you and let's see if the connection clears up.

Shawn switches seats with Leona and now sits with Dr. Theo across from her on the spirit board.

Shawn: Who is here, is it Heroditus?
Unseen friend: Yes. I am Heroditus. May I explain?
Dr. Theo and **Shawn:** Yes, please do!
Heroditus: I was the one on earlier, but the student's consciousness is simply not acclimated to this technology. This is OK - Because her

connection with her guide is strong in other ways. Celebrate that!
Dr. Theo: Heroditus, I can connect quickly with my sister on the board, even though she has not done as much deep spiritual work. However, we connect easily every time we focus on the board. Others, such as clients and friends I have used this method of communication with to reach you or Tony, have been difficult at first, but it eventually smooths out. Is the connection dependent on past lives, multidimensional connection, and the connection to who is on the other side willing to come through and help?
Heroditus: Absolutely, and some people cannot do it. Think of how certain people are good at sports – and others have no coordination. Some brains and minds are simply not compatible for this method of communication. Shawn's ability can usually override another's board limitations. You have a special connection with your sister – that's an exception.
Dr. Theo: Excellent clarification, thank you Heroditus.
Shawn: Thank you so much for this. Good night Heroditus!
Heroditus: Always a joy! Goodbye!

Wednesday, November 15, 2017 8:45 PM
Spirit Board session. Dr. Theo with his sister Teresa; Teresa's residence.

Dr. Theo states his affirmation invocation and the session begins.

Dr. Theo: Who's here with guidance today?
Unseen friend: Tony.
Teresa: Tony, why am I having this headache?
Tony: Take an aspirin.
Teresa: How many?
Tony: Two. Nourish. Buy healthy foods.
Dr. Theo: Why has my left eyelid been twitching for a week straight?
Tony: You are not sleeping enough.
Dr. Theo: I've been working hard on the projects, how's it looking from your perspective - my sleep quality?
Tony: Horrible.
Dr. Theo: Is this radio show going to have any movement? There's lots of stress around the organization.

Tony: Just have fun. That is all that matters.
Dr. Theo: There has been such funky energy the last two weeks, things feel off.
Tony: The Devil is working.
Dr. Theo: Tony, I do not believe the Devil is strong enough to overpower the light of God.
Tony: Correct. Yes, but he tries. Be vigilant.
Dr. Theo: Is there some ominous event that the dark is preparing for, to throw against the world. More false flag attacks, and fear mongering news reports?
Tony: Always. But do not fear.
Dr. Theo: Tony, I don't. We try not to. I feel so grateful for your presence and guidance, thank you. Goodbye for now.
Tony: Goodbye.

Monday, December 18, 2017 8:16 PM
Spirit Board session. Dr. Theo with his sister Teresa; Teresa's residence.

Dr. Theo states his affirmation invocation and the session begins.

Dr. Theo: Who is with us?

Planchette has immediate connection, moves in a circular pattern and starts forming words.

Unseen friend: Tony.
Dr. Theo and **Teresa:** Hello Tony! We're happy you are here with us.
Tony: Greetings once more, very happy to be here as well.
Dr. Theo: So, Tony I want to ask you today about romance. I am so tired of the lack of substance in many of today's women. I yearn for the deep true love I know exists and deserve. And I know there is a lot I have to do before I focus on manifesting that. Can you tell me at least, if she's out there, who to look for? What is her name? I know there are many potentials and free will exists, it can go in many directions. I know this. Also asking you takes away some of the surprise of the event when it happens, but I am willing to

at this moment know, I ask to know. Can you please describe her so when I see her, I will know it is her without question?
Tony: You will know.
Dr. Theo: How?
Tony: You will feel like you never felt before.
Dr. Theo: I'm so looking forward to that Tony.
Tony: In her 30's, and yes, she does have blue eyes.
Dr. Theo: (Laughing) yes, you know me too well - I do love those blue eyes. Does she have any brothers or sisters?
Tony: One older brother.
Dr. Theo: Where or how do I meet her?
Tony: By chance.
Dr. Theo: Will this be the true love I have waited for in life?
Tony: Yes.
Dr. Theo: So how long before I meet this lovely woman? I know time is not real and you cannot really give me a time per free will and things can always change, including this - but approximately?
Tony: Yes, this can change, all free will. Approximately two years your time.
Dr. Theo: Okay so what do I do for two years? Can I date around?
Tony: Focus on your personal development. Free will. If you want to waste your time and money go date around.
Dr. Theo: (Laughing) Yes, good point. Thank you. On the topic of health, I have been coughing for a while now since the California fires hit nearby Brentwood. It seems to be getting worse, can you tell me what's going on? How much longer will this cough last?
Tony: One more month.
Dr. Theo: What! Oh my God! Why? It's already been two weeks.
Tony: Respiratory infection. Your lack of proper sleep, and physical care has caught up with you. The smoke in the air had poison from the fires; you inhaled and this caused your current condition. Long hours at the office and staying up late for over 3 months straight, was not wise.
Dr. Theo: Oh my God, you did warn me about the sleep yes.
Tony: Correct. You are not Superman.
Dr. Theo: (Laughing) I do think I am though at times Tony.
Tony: You're not. Take care of your body.

Dr. Theo: Okay seriously now, what can I do to get rid of this quickly?
Tony: You know already. Sleep, pure healing juices, and Z-pack or alternative. It will clear in time.
Dr. Theo: Thank you for the information Tony, sometimes the healer needs the healing advice. So, my sister now wants to know about her special someone.
Teresa: Yes! What is the guy's name I'm going to marry and is he Greek?
Tony: Petros, Yes Greek.

Teresa's face goes into a blank stare.

Dr. Theo: What's wrong?
Teresa: Nothing. I have to ask this, what's his age?
Tony: 46.
Teresa: No way!
Dr. Theo: What?
Teresa: I'm now talking to someone online and his name is Petros, he's Greek and he's 46. Wait, I need to know if this is really the same guy, Tony - what does he do for a living and where does he live?
Tony: Executive of a company. Lives in Arcadia.
Teresa: Wow, yes this is the same guy! We've been talking online for two weeks but will meet up soon.
Dr. Theo: My mind is totally blown right now! Ask and you SHALL receive! So, the same guy Tony is describing, happens to be the same guy you're going to date and may be married to? Amazing!
Tony: Free will. Life choices. Many possibilities.
Dr. Theo: Yes, that's true sis, you can choose not to and another opportunity will come - everything is free will that changes with each thought and choice.
Tony: Correct.
Dr. Theo: So let me ask this Tony... is there a question we haven't asked that we should be asking?
Tony: To be or not to be?
Teresa: Is that the question? Are you being serious?
Tony: No. Ha-ha. A Joke.

Dr. Theo: I see you're back to your humor Tony, nice. Okay, so I have had lots of communication issues with my friend since the show began. Seems we're not on the same page artistically. I am feeling it is in my best interest to host this show alone, without a co-host; any thoughts?
Tony: Do as you please, live your life.
Dr. Theo: And with that, we will close this session, it has been quite an evening of reveals. As always, very grateful and humbled for our co-creation of energy here.
Teresa: Thank you and good night Tony.
Tony: Yes indeed. IC-XC-NI-KA Goodbye.

Tuesday, January 9, 2018 7:30 PM
Spirit Board session. Dr. Theo with his sister Teresa; Teresa's residence.

Dr. Theo states his affirmation invocation and the session begins.

Dr. Theo: Who is with us?
Unseen friend: Tony.
Dr. Theo and **Teresa:** Hello Tony!
Tony: A pleasure always.
Teresa: Tony can you tell me why an older woman, a new patient, while at work in the hospital today came into my life all of a sudden?
Tony: To bring you joy. A new friend.
Teresa: She's so full of life! She's a senior but has the energy of a 40-year-old, very refreshing. She is very wise as well. So, Tony I must know why I have difficulty with dating. Men always let me down. I went out with Petros and I had high expectations, but he's a recovering alcoholic, smoker, and between jobs right now! Not exactly what I was expecting as a perfect match.
Dr. Theo: So, he's human eh? (Laughing) No one's perfect sis. Let's give the guy credit for changing his life around and becoming a better person. Tony, I think she's frustrated and wants to know what her MAIN issue is with dating.
Tony: Teresa has commitment issues.
Teresa: Well yes, I know that, but why is it I do?
Dr. Theo: Because you love the challenge of having what you can't get! Women love the guys they can't have - or which make themselves

unavailable. Once the guy tells you he's dedicated to you and happens to be a great catch, you gals make them just a friend.
Tony: Right.
Teresa: True, yes that is how it was with my previous relationship. I knew he wasn't committing so I wanted him more. I thought that I could get him to change his mind. Must be a subconscious thing, so what can I do?
Tony: Stop being so picky. You are not perfect either.
Dr. Theo: Yes, everyone has somewhere to improve; I feel you're blocking love by looking for perfection.
Tony: She has to decide if she wants to be with him. Her choices.
Teresa: Okay, let's say I don't pick him, who am I meeting probably in the next few weeks?
Tony: An Egyptian man.
Teresa: What's his name?
Tony: Be open.
Dr. Theo: Wait a minute sis, you're going to repeat the past by not learning the lesson here. Tony does Petros feel Teresa is a possible life partner for him? Does he fancy her as a future bride, and mother of his kids?
Tony: Yes.
Dr. Theo: So now you know, there's potential there. Your move!
Teresa: I don't know, I need to sort through all my feelings here, you ask your questions.
Dr. Theo: Okay yes, fair enough. Tony, I have questions surrounding this random letter I received in February from an unknown woman who claims I came to her in a dream, around the time my channeling and deeper work with you and Heroditus began. This is the third time within the last two years someone told me they saw a very vivid dream of me teaching them how to heal or been spontaneously healed themselves. I get emotional reading the letter and want to know what this is all about. She saw and wrote some amazing things I felt true since I was a child and she foresaw future events. Why did I get this letter from her?
Tony: To keep you moving forward in life and your healing practice.
Dr. Theo: I admit, yes, I was feeling serious doubts at the time about my direction, I thought I was going for lack of better terms, crazy. My perception of reality really began to change and it alarmed me. It is amazing

to know that this letter came to reassure me when I needed it most and now I know things are true as they are. So, the healings she mentions in the letter are future events that are to occur? My healing abilities are to become so powerful?

Tony: Very possible. You will touch many on a grand scale.

Dr. Theo: (I was shocked at his words and found it hard to answer but finally found my voice and said:) I'm speechless and am about to explode with tears of joy. This I have felt and known as my truth as a child, seen it in visions - I just never knew exactly when or how. This is a lot to take in right now. Thank you so much for the validations.

Tony: Your children will prophesy and heal. Love will light the world.

Dr. Theo: (By this time, I was wiping away tears:) Should I start a church, or group, how should I continue?

Tony: No. Too many churches. Too little speak the truth. Jesus said to Peter, "Peter you are my rock, and on this rock, I will build my church. Inside of you all lies my church."

Dr. Theo: Then what is the next logical step for me to take in this mission?

Tony: It will unfold as time flies.

Dr. Theo: Tony, is there anyone else that I know of outside of you, Heroditus, my Uncle Tony, my grandparents, extended family on the other side, that heals with me? Who else will help me with such a huge task, I want to know everyone's names! Who will help me heal the people!?

Tony: Jesus.

Dr. Theo: Tony did I know Jesus in a past life, am I in some way connected? It feels so.

Tony: He is with you all the time. All are part of the whole.

Dr. Theo: True, we are all connected, all we need to do is use our heart and mind to connect. I want to learn how to be in this 'space' more often. I am in a state of glowing love and enthusiasm, deep gratefulness, humbled to have had this discussion today. This is a lot to process. Thank you so much! Are any of our guides or relatives wishing to communicate at this time with us?

Tony: No, none at this time.

Dr. Theo: Any words of wisdom before we depart for today Tony?

Tony: Love and light always. IC XC NI KA, goodbye.

Dr. Theo and **Teresa:** Amen, good night.

Saturday, January 13, 2018 3:30 PM
Spirit Board session. Dr. Theo with his sister Teresa; Teresa's residence.

Dr. Theo states his affirmation invocation and the session begins.

Dr. Theo: Who is with us?
Unseen friend: Tony.
Dr. Theo and **Teresa:** Hello Tony!
Tony: Delighted to be here with you this fine day!
Dr. Theo: Tony, yes indeed it is a beautiful day outside, sunny and warm. I have several important questions to ask, Thursday was an interesting day. I feel I need to get confirmation today on what I experienced. I was a guest on a friend's radio show. It was the first time I publicly spoke about my faith, angelic guides and Christ's power in healing work. Throughout the show my mic went dead, and at one point all mics in the studio went dead which interrupted the show. Management had to come in and figure out what was going on and fix it. In the year or so that the host had her radio program, this had never happened. It just so happened at that time and that moment. Was this random, or not?
Tony: Frustrating wasn't it?
Dr. Theo: YES! That's exactly what I was feeling - frustration, but I was still calm, very calm - and in me I KNEW this was a spiritual attack. Was I right?
Tony: This is dark energy. Darkness does not like the light and tries all it can to put it out.
Dr. Theo: I knew I was going to be fine. I knew it all was going to be fixed. I felt a presence and a protection in the room the whole time. What is this presence, this knowing? Where does it come from?
Tony: The subconscious.
Dr. Theo: Yes, but what is it? Is it faith? My belief? What is it?
Tony: Light force.
Dr. Theo: And is this light force basically God inside?
Tony: Yes. Knowing. Gnosis.
Dr. Theo: Thank you for this clarification. It helps to know what I was

feeling and to connect the two. Okay, so can you please tell me what is going on between the light and the dark? Is it a yin and yang? Why did the light allow the dark to even get a chance to mess with the microphones? I remember when I performed the exorcism at the house not long ago, dark energy was messing with the owner of the house as well as the camera operator videotaping the event. The dark tried to cut off the camera from working so we couldn't expose it.

Tony: The battle is constant.

Dr. Theo: Why did that happen at the station? I knew instinctively it was dark forces. I heard it as an echo, vibration in my head, not like someone who says it and you hear it with your ears, but instead as a knowing, an internal hearing. Who was it that told me this?

Tony: Your angel. Always with you. This was just a small example.

Dr. Theo: Which angel?

Tony: David.

Dr. Theo: Oh wow, can you tell me more about David? I do not know of a David as an Archangel.

Tony: No, he is an angel.

Dr. Theo: I didn't know I had an angel named David with me, what is his function to me?

Tony: Guard. He is one of many.

Dr. Theo: Can you please give me the names of all my guardian angels?

Tony: No. Far too many.

Dr. Theo: Okay I understand. After that event occurred at the radio station, I went to a business meeting to see if an agent, or talent representative, would be a good fit with helping me get the healing message out to the world. Once I walked into his office it felt very uninviting. It was dark, old magazines laid around in a piled mess and the waiting room was empty with only a couch in it. The energy in there was very cold and heavy. When I met him, his face wore the sadness and pain of lifetimes on it. He spoke with me and I got to know him. It didn't take long for him to tell me that he was an atheist and that he believed Jesus Christ is as real as the tooth fairy. At this point I felt my senses become sharpened and I noticed vibrant details. He would talk normally and at times his tone changed when I brought up Christianity and Jesus. I heard a voice internally again tell me, "This is what you will be up against. This type of energy. This type of thinking." I could see through his eyes what was inside and controlling him, and felt so sorry for him, as I felt love for the human trapped inside. I knew at that point we were not a good match to work together, but I prayed that he finds his way to the light for healing. As I walked out he stopped me and asked if I could help heal his frozen right shoulder. I offered to feel and touch it to see how much scar tissue hindered his movement. As I was taking his shoulder through the range of movement, a thought came to me, reminding me of the woman who received her miracle of movement in an expo not long ago for the same exact symptoms he was asking healing for. The difference was she was a believer, and he wasn't. I told him this, and it went in one ear and out the other. I left the office feeling drained, and sad about the obvious plight of his thinking keeping him from healing and how blind he was to finding the truth.

Tony: He is a negative force. It is not in your highest good to work with him, although you have free will. His mind is plagued with many negativities. Yahweh was crucified. You will be too if you follow the truth.

Dr. Theo: Wow. Why must good people who follow the truth and the light end up dying for these principles?

Tony: Love.

Dr. Theo: Are some people just born evil then? Some people are just full of hate?

Tony: No. Evil is a choice.

Dr. Theo: So, what about the young souls, babies who come into the world for five or six years, maybe even weeks or days only and die so soon - prior to even making any choices or committing evil acts? Are these poor souls marked as evil by God when they return to the other side?

Tony: No, they are freed.

Dr. Theo: So, do these souls come in to serve as a purpose or lesson to those who are living? Or are they coming in to bodies to strictly experience what it's like to die at the hands of a murderer solely for the life or traumatic experience? Or both?

Tony: All is choice of free will.

Dr. Theo: Seems to be the gift and the curse of duality. Speaking of which, I have two personal relations companies I am considering on hiring. I know

I have to make my own choices and decisions, but I want to ask if it is in my highest good to hire a PR company at this time and which one?
Tony: No. Not at this time.
Dr. Theo: So, what do I do to grow my business then? What is in my highest good for growth?
Tony: Nothing, you do just as you are. You will be guided.
Dr. Theo: Sis, don't you have questions today?
Teresa: No, these answers to your questions are very fascinating, I'm just here to learn and for support right now. Lots to digest!
Dr. Theo: Okay, thank you so much for the clarification and insight Tony, as always - it's a blessing to have higher counsel with our beloved unseen friends. With this we end our session for now, goodbye.
Teresa: Goodbye Tony.
Tony: Goodbye.

Thursday, February 1, 2018 1:00 PM
Dr. Theo and Shawn; Shawn's office. Spirit board - Recorded session.

Shawn states her affirmation invocation and the session begins. Planchette moves immediately, connecting with Heroditus.

Unseen friend: Back with you, Theo, on the board is a joy. Of course, Heroditus is here.
Dr. Theo: So, this is Heroditus speaking? Hello again my friend.
Heroditus: Yes. Question, for we know you have many.
Dr. Theo: Oh yes, I always do. (Laughing) Well the first question concerns my mother and parents. Every year when they come into town for two months I am afflicted with some physical mystery ailment that comes out of nowhere. This year it's a really bad chest congestion and cough that started right before their visit. Triggered by the fires, though still is lingering but should have cleared a while ago. It got better with my father's flight out two weeks ago but it's still here. My mother is still in town and I feel the same thing as last year will occur. Last year as soon as they came into town my neck went into spasm and I got an MRI that showed two bulging discs

which was a similar issue that I had when my left arm became paralyzed earlier in my youth! Once they both left town last February, the pain immediately lifted. However, the whole time they were in town, the pain lingered with no relief in sight until they both left to the other side of the country again. Do they trigger something in me?

Heroditus: The body is reflecting old deeper conflicts with parents. They still represent a certain discomfort with their beliefs which impinge on your chosen freedom of spiritual development - which includes the more esoteric aspects of your work which you are so passionate about.

Shawn: Heroditus, are you saying there is a friction subconsciously?

Heroditus: Yes. Subconscious friction. So, it will be important to meditate to deep levels to cut and totally sever the cords of constraint. Your love for them will grow afterwards as your deeper sense of freedom takes hold within you.

Dr. Theo: Interesting he says deep levels, as this morning after getting out of the shower, I was thinking about the conversation I needed to have with them, specifically my mother, and a sharp deep pain struck me in the middle of my back suddenly without reason, and I couldn't breathe. Right now, I'm still feeling it. Feels as if rib heads or thoracic vertebrae are badly subluxated.

Heroditus: A past life with mother that is coming up to show you how deep the hidden inner cords of conflict are rooted.

Shawn: The interesting thing here is you say it's a rib head; like Adam and Eve, the man and woman energy reflection.

Dr. Theo: Heroditus, I'd like to know if this is connected to the past life with her that another reader told me about years ago. She said that we were married in ancient Greece and she had betrayed me by leaving me to be with a Persian king who tempted her away from me with promises of fortunes, gems and rubies from his lands. Since youth, I can remember that I never cared for shiny fancy things either, and I look down on overt flashy materialism. In this lifetime we agreed I'd be her son, to make it up to me and nurture me, which explains her doting over me as her 'favorite' through my childhood and always making sure I was happy.

Heroditus: Now she feels you are leaving her.

Shawn: So Heroditus this deep meditation of cutting cords can really help him see her in a better light? How often do you recommend he meditate and how?

Heroditus: Cut the cords daily for one week then once a week for at least 6 months. Visualize her standing opposite you with both forms past and present life. Tell her what you are going to do and that it will increase a healthy love between you. State: "I love you and release us to our greater divine selves."

Dr. Theo: As far as helping other people to release their bonds, is this something I can bring to my clients for any relationship, not only familial?

Heroditus: Yes. First however, they need to understand the contract forged into the unconscious and how it is mutual.

Shawn: He's saying that your clients will have to understand that they are a participant in the mutual making of their choices and decisions, not something that has been just done to them. That may be hard for some people to understand.

Dr. Theo: Speaking of patients, I have an emergency call that came in just before we sat down for this session. A client is needing help with healing of her knee. She can't walk and claims she must work a full day on her feet tomorrow in court. She is hoping I can bring her back to 100% for her trial. Can you give me any insight on the root of her situation?

Heroditus: Brace; a meaningful metaphor for her. Brace and be braced. And be willing to receive help. Stay on your own two feet but let bracing be with you.

Shawn: So, he's saying in her life she needs to feel supported, not just in her work but also in her deeper personal life's meaning.

Heroditus: Yes, bigger theme for her.

Dr. Theo: Thank you Heroditus. I can physically work with her but also emotionally. This wisdom can help her gain more inner strength.

Heroditus: A strengthening and preparation for difficult encounters.

Dr. Theo: Excellent thank you for this, I know it will help her. Since we are still on the topic of healing, I want to talk about Jesus Christ. Can you please tell me more about him? I want to know why I feel I am so connected to him. Did we have a connection when He was on this Earth?

Heroditus: It would seem so, but the lifetime you had during his time was one in which you had visons of Jesus which were very, very real to you as if you were physically with him. But not physically geographically close. You did see him once physically.

Dr. Theo: I have this feeling that I was some sort of disciple or follower during that time.

Shawn: Yes, you seem to have been a fan of what was being said and happening around that time and had visions during that time. Heroditus, were these visions projections from Jesus? Was he projecting his power to others?

Heroditus: Yes.

Shawn: Interesting, he had a very psychic connection with his people.

Dr. Theo: Heroditus, what was I doing in that time, was I a follower of the teachings of Christ as the word was being spread?

Heroditus: You had a family to feed so you had to stay and work in your village – a cobbler.

Shawn: Wow, this is interesting so you had to stay and weren't able as a cobbler to leave everything and follow. Cobblers also have a lot of time in meditation, so a lot of that psychic meditation must have been nurtured.

Dr. Theo: I feel a lot of that ability is coming back to light now, and it's very exciting.

Heroditus: This time stay more grounded than the past life was.

Dr. Theo: Heroditus, I have questions about the miracles of Jesus and being able to use his name to heal people as happened with the lady in the seminar who could not raise her arm, but after I spoke the name of Christ she was able to. She was able to reach her alternate space of healing. Yet another man, a non-believer who recently came to me with the same issue – asked I look at his shoulder. For him nothing happened even though I did the same exact thing for him that I did for the woman. When will the power work? What is the structure if I may ask? Even some of Christ's own disciples were unable to remove infirmities in his name as written in Matthew 17:14. What blocks the power and what unlocks it? If someone has total faith, will healing always be given to them?

Heroditus: Depends. The consciousness of others can be confusing sometimes. There are no guaranteed formulas for what can co-create a miracle. But sometimes things can line up.

Dr. Theo: So, is there any way we can help things line up? Is it when everyone is in communication, in likeminded-ness? When two of more minds are together, He is with us? Is that the idea, as said in the Bible?

Heroditus: When invited, His healing love can be present. Invite from your purest self.

Dr. Theo: So, although no guarantees, it would have to be everyone inviting from their purest selves. Heroditus, I am not in any way pure, and in no way sinless, and in no way perfect. So as an imperfect person, how can I still be able to do these things? Am I, in my imperfections, still worthy enough to be able to give a loving message from above?

Heroditus: Of course! And striving to step back to allow certain energies to flow through you.

Dr. Theo: Heroditus, I want to bring much more spiritual power into my work; should I just go for it during sessions with clients? What do you suggest?

Heroditus: Ask the individuals to share their spiritual beliefs with you openly. Then adjust your vocabulary accordingly.

Dr. Theo: Wise. How do I know my present teacher in channeling, Shawn Randall. What is the past life connection here?

Heroditus: As members of a secret order like the Rosicrucians. Both of you were mediums.

Shawn: How interesting! I've always felt I must have been a medium in a former life. So, there you go. Heroditus, how can Theo strengthen his connection with you outside of classes, and the board work?

Heroditus: When you talk with Tony - your uncle - ask for me to join you openly. Your mind will be in 'concrete connection mode'. Tony has been training with you - so, in that asking moment shift over to me! Like changing channels on a TV.

Shawn: You have a very strong energy with your Uncle Tony. So, using that connection you can ask Tony to bring Heroditus in at that moment. How beautiful, I love the 'concrete connection' phrase!

Dr. Theo: Heroditus, I have a question on the things 'energy Tony' told me that are to come with healings. How do I connect to my healing team on the other side to do this larger mass healing work? Tony told me that I just need to ask for Jesus and he will be there to help. Can you tell me about the

healing team on the other side that is working with me?
Heroditus: There are other healers in spirit that attend with you in healing sessions. But they do not wish to share their names.
Shawn: I want to note that they moved the planchette to the 'all that is' space. When they do this, it means the unseen friends wish to amplify their message on the point they are making. So, Heroditus is saying that it may not be important for you to know their names relative to your growth at this time and to just know the power is there with you during your sessions.
Dr. Theo: Understood. Yes. I'd like to change the topic to current events. Our society seems to be moving forward with transparency in many areas, such as cleaning up politics and the uncovering of classified government secrets by whistleblowers. Recently there have been a lot of reports that much of the moon and space travel videos are forged using CGI, greenscreens, and they Photoshop images to keep everyone in the dark. Is NASA lying to the public?
Heroditus: NASA believes they should only reveal information that they understand and can explain - they want to protect average citizens from inaccurate assumptions and fears that NASA feels would be damaging. They also want to protect their image.
Dr. Theo: So, this must mean they have seen much that is outside the current human understanding, and they themselves can't present the information in a way that they feel people can handle. It would be a huge paradigm shift for us. Many however feel that not telling people what they know keeps humanity ignorant, and that's also not a good thing. Seems they are in a very challenging position.
Shawn: Indeed, if they themselves are ignorant of what they are witnessing, it would be tough to explain it without frightening the public. Also, they don't want to look ignorant in front of the public as they are supposed to be the experts of space. I do love how Heroditus explains it, as he is very neutral and non-judgmental in his answer's wording. There is no negative intent, depending on the person asking the question. Perspective is key.
Dr. Theo: Why is there such secrecy with Antarctica? What is going on down there at the pole?
Heroditus: Deeply dangerous zones and experiments taking place.
Dr. Theo: So, what are they doing exactly? Do tell!

Heroditus: Zip.
Dr. Theo and **Shawn**: (Laughing)
Dr. Theo: Oh, come on Heroditus! Are you not telling us for our own protection?
Heroditus: Zip, Zip.
Shawn: How funny, he's keeping his lips sealed on this one. They may be experimenting with the magnetic fields. Sometimes entities will not give information that does not help your life mission. This may be one of those times.
Heroditus: So, dear human of mine Theo, keep reaching out to me telepathically. And writing with me is still recommendable. We love you deeply, goodbye.
Dr. Theo: Love you all as well, thank you very much, goodbye!
Shawn: Goodbye Heroditus!

Sunday, February 12, 4:00 PM
Spirit board session. Dr. Theo with his sister Teresa; Dr. Theo's office.

Dr. Theo states his affirmation invocation and the session begins.

Dr. Theo: Who is with us?
Unseen friend: Tony.
Dr. Theo: Thank you for being with us Tony, I'd like to ask right off the bat a question for my mother. She wonders who her Archangel is, can you tell me?
Tony: Raphael protects her.
Dr. Theo: Concerning a holy woman called St. Anastasia in Greece who my mother has followed for decades and saw the vision for me after my first months of life; would it be in my mother's highest good to volunteer, work and live there with the organization? She's thinking about staying there in her senior years.
Tony: Yes, the organization is with the light.
Dr. Theo: Can I give my mother any information to help her uplift her mood?
Tony: You can't force her to be happy.
Dr. Theo: Yes, I tell her all the time that she has to choose happiness.

Tony: Yes.

Dr. Theo: Tony can you please tell me how I can best work with the PR company I just hired. I went with my intuition and so far, I'm pleased.

Tony: Follow your gut. Put all your energy into your work.

Dr. Theo: Okay, how is everything going from your side concerning the creation of hypnotherapy audio sessions with clients?

Tony: Yes, well.

Dr. Theo: Beautiful, glad to hear that, I'm excited about the impact it will have. I'd like some insight on a patient that is abusing drugs for years but feels he has it all under control. He toys with the idea of stopping use. How can I help him further? I feel the loop closing work done with my method to recondition his nervous system is improving his life, but how can I go deeper?

Tony: It has. However, he has to - want - to stop doing drugs.

Dr. Theo: What is he getting from the drugs, there's always a payoff, or a deeper agreement within one self - what is his payoff?

Tony: He enjoys living a parallel life in the moment with no responsibilities.

Dr. Theo: Makes perfect sense. How can I help him further?

Tony: Just be an ear.

Dr. Theo: I have another patient who can't stop gossiping. What insight for her?

Tony: Gossip is her escape from her own reality. She will learn her lesson on her own.

Teresa: Tony, I have a question; we used to astral travel a lot as a kids, how can we do it again more often?

Tony: Prayer can do wonders.

Dr. Theo: So, you're saying we should ask our angels to help?

Tony: Yes.

Dr. Theo: Tony, is fasting like people do it these days correct? There's so much misinformation as to what is good for the body, any recommendations from the light?

Tony: You should eat as God commanded in the Old Testament. Stay away from foods not clean for you.

Teresa: What! Oh No! Tony, I love shrimp even though it's supposedly unclean!

Tony: Free will. You may eat it, but not good for you, not highest vibration.
Dr. Theo: I see, certain animals are for other animals in the food chain, humans should eat the proper foods as described in Old Testament for best health. This makes perfect sense if we look at the diseases affecting the masses. Incorrect foods lead to everything from allergies to chronic diseases.
Tony: Follow the light. Follow God's word.
Teresa: We have a question about a man who we both know a long time. He talks a lot about God and has prophesized events that occurred, but something doesn't seem right. Is he with the light?
Tony: No. Stay away, he is possessed and thinks he is working with the light.
Teresa: I knew it! I felt it. He was involved with a sorceress of sorts long ago.
Dr. Theo: Tony, how can we tell if someone is possessed? People will always point the finger at someone or something they don't understand or fear and yell 'devil!' Channeling and spirit boards also fall into that category for the unexperienced fearful minds. They even said that of Jesus too; claiming his miracles were the work of demons and he could heal people only because he was of the same energy that he was casting out. So, how to easily spot the difference?
Tony: Ego. The one you speak of craves attention. No helping of others. Just attention.
Dr. Theo: Ah. I see. The intention and the deeds will always tell us. As in Matthew, A good tree produces good fruit, and a bad tree produces bad fruit.
Tony: Yes.
Dr. Theo: Tony, I received a nasty random email message from someone Thursday. It really took me by surprise. The guy who wrote this seemed seriously irrational, emotional and delusional in his message. It felt very hateful. As I began to read it a wave of negativity felt like it was penetrating through me, and I immediately felt very weak and dizzy. I had to just stop and lay down. As I prayed I got home and took a deep mineral bath to get my mind off it. I felt better but was shocked at how it came at me like that. It was very similar to the time I confronted a possessed woman at a bus stop by praying for her; only to have her lash out and try to scratch my eyes out.

When I was focused, her negativity could not touch me. However, once I lost focus even for one second she scratched the tip of my nose and the bad vibes were palpable for days.
Tony: Demon energy of the lowest vibration. Immediately say the Jesus Prayer.
Dr. Theo: 'Lord Jesus Christ, Son of God, have mercy on me, a sinner', while praying repeatedly with depth, humility and love in heart and mind?
Tony: Yes.
Dr. Theo: So, I feel I am protected and I understand I am a child of God as you have said - we all are, but why was I affected like that? It was horrible. I could actually feel the wave of dark energy come through the computer monitor at me, it was so tangible. When you're sensitive, you can feel these vibrations.
Tony: Just a small taste of what Yahweh went through and what you will face if you take the path.
Dr. Theo: How can I stop it from ever affecting me like that in the future?
Tony: You are to feel. You are human. Say the Jesus Prayer. IC-XC-NI-KA.
Dr. Theo: Tony, tell me what exactly I am getting into here?
Tony: No. Free will. Live your life.
Dr. Theo: I understand. Telling me certain things before their time, could in fact create a new reality from my current point of perception, and remove me from a path that may grow me the way I am to grow. You do not want to manipulate my free will. I thank you for that.
Tony: Correct.
Dr. Theo: I remember as a teenager - during the years I was bullied, asking to live a life that is unparalleled – wanting to lift the pain of others. I have been through so much, yet I feel it's all only just begun. I am looking forward to more. I want the most out of this life.
Tony: Do what you love.

At this moment I felt a wave of love and deep peace go through me.

Dr. Theo: Tony, I love God, and I love people. I just want to be part of something spectacular, let God work through me, shine His glory.
Tony: "Then pick up your cross and follow me."

Dr. Theo: (Tearfully) Thank you so much Tony for your message.
Tony: IC XC NI KA, Goodbye.
Teresa: Goodbye Tony.
Tony: Goodbye.

This entry marks the end of the first year of communication with my guides through board work. There was massive growth and understanding for me within this time that clarified and tied together many of my life's events.

Note: It is important one does much 'inner' personal development prior to using the board (or any tool) for Spirit communication. Also, proper instruction from an experienced, high frequency light worker is vital for safe communication. This cannot be understated.

I hope this dialogue and the previous chapters have helped you learn what a healthy and high version of channeling Spirit looks like.

Conclusion

"There are two types of people on this earth; a Sack of bones dragging a soul or a Soul carrying a sack of bones."
~ Efrat Cybulkiewicz

There has been so much more loving communion shared with my guides since the publication of this book. For me the *connection* with my guides continues to be one of the most amazing experiences of my life. I thank all my mentors, especially Shawn Randall whose personalized instruction helped me unlock my communication with my personal guides. Channeling continues to deepen my knowing that there is far more to God's wonderous creation than what we see just with our physical eyes.

It is with massive gratitude for spirit's guidance in which I finish the words in this book. As I reflect on the events that have transpired throughout my life, remembering the choices, events, and 'coincidences', that strike pure awe in me, I cannot offer enough thanks to the Divine higher team of 'self' we all have connection to - IF we choose to open it, learn from it, and move with it.

I hope you have the chance to connect with your heavenly hosts. I wish that you find your truth from your own inner asking and are led to it by the Divine love by which we are all created. As always, we cannot make someone find 'God' - we can only do our best to connect ourselves to the light and let it shine so that others wish to seek their path as well.

In the highest vibration of love and light - God bless,

See you at the seminars!

Theodoros Kousouli D.C., CHt.

About the Author

A holistic health care advisor, teacher, speaker, mentor and author who is featured on major networks, Theodoros Kousouli D.C., CHt., is Los Angeles' premier holistic metaphysical energy healer. He is recognized and trusted for effective, quick, drug-free results. His remarkable natural, pain-free, holistic healing system - the Kousouli® Method - focuses on getting patients to their top performance levels by unblocking pathways using the body's own repair mechanisms. His desire to help others stems from his personal journey recovering from semi-paralysis and major heart surgeries and includes everything he's learned about the optimum wellness techniques that define his practice.

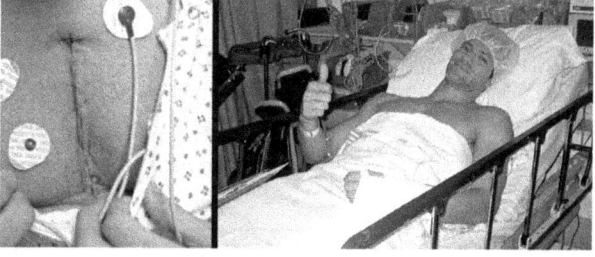

Dr. Theo Kousouli is the author of *the Be A Master® Series (BeAMaster.Com)*, including: *BE A MASTER® of PSYCHIC ENERGY and BE A MASTER® of MAXIMUM HEALING*. A personal coach and advisor to entertainers, business leaders, energy healers, and spiritual seekers of all varieties, Dr. Kousouli holds seminars teaching people how to tap into their inner healing and higher-level abilities through the use of their nervous systems. Visit **www.KousouliMethod.com** for more information on developing your intuition and personal power to live a more purpose-filled, meaningful, and healthy life. Dr. Kousouli is the ideal speaker for your next event.

To Schedule Dr. Theo Kousouli For Your Next Event:
www.DrKousouli.com

Be A Master® Of Channeling Spirit

Life Changing Products · Books · Seminars · Empowerment Audios · Get on the Newsletter!
Connect with Dr. Kousouli, www.DrKousouli.com @DrKousouli #DrKousouli #KousouliMethod
You Will Also Enjoy Dr. Kousouli's Other Published Works. Available Now from Major Retailers:

BE A MASTER® OF MAXIMUM HEALING
How to Lead a Healthy Life Without Limits
- Holistic Solutions for over 60 Diseases to Help You and Your Loved Ones Heal!

BE A MASTER® OF PSYCHIC ENERGY
Your Key to Truly Mastering Your Personal Power
- Uncover and Amplify Your Hidden Psychic Abilities to Change Your Life!

BE A MASTER® OF SEX ENERGY
Hypnotize Your Partner for Love and Great Sex
- Build a Stronger Bond with Your Lover(s) Using Subconscious Science!

BE A MASTER® OF SUCCESS
Dr. Kousouli's 33 Master Secrets to Achieving Your Dreams
- Solid Success Principles You Can Apply Right Now to Empower Your Life!

BE A MASTER® OF SELF IMAGE
Dr. Kousouli's 33 Master Secrets to Living Healthier, Happier and Hotter
- Simple Holistic Tips & Tricks for More Weight Loss and Body Benefit to You!

BE A MASTER® OF SELF LOVE
Dr. Kousouli's 33 Master Secrets to Loving Your Extraordinary Life
- Overcome Bullying, Abuse, Depression and Build Massive Self-Esteem & Self-Love!

BE A MASTER® OF YOUR REALITY
Authentically Manifest Your Desires
- Use the Law of Attraction to Radically Transform Your Life!

If you would like to share your story of how Dr. Kousouli's books, audios or seminars have impacted your life for the better, we would love to hear from you!

For A Free Gift from Dr. Theo Kousouli visit www.FreeGiftFromDrTheo.com

www.ingramcontent.com/pod-product-compliance
Lightning Source LLC
Chambersburg PA
CBHW080543170426
43195CB00016B/2656